The *Christmas Strawberry*

...and Other Stories

Also by Beth Lindsay Templeton

Loving Our Neighbor: A Thoughtful Approach to Helping People in Poverty

Understanding Poverty in the Classroom: Changing Perceptions for Student Success

Angelika's Journal: What You Can Do about Poverty and Homelessness

A Coat Named Mr. Spot

Conversations on the Porch: Ancient Voices—Contemporary Wisdom

More Conversations on the Porch: Ancient Voices—Contemporary Wisdom

Refrigerator Prayers for Ordinary People

Uncharted Journey: Getting Older and Other Life Transitions

Beth Lindsay Templeton

The Christmas Strawberry
...and Other Stories

FpS

Greenville, South Carolina

The Christmas Strawberry
...and Other Stories

Copyright © 2017-2018 Beth Lindsay Templeton

All rights reserved. No part of this book may be used of reproduced by any means, graphic, electronic, or mechanical, including photocopying, recording, taping or by any information storage retrieval without the written permission of the publisher except in the case of brief quotations embodied in critical articles and reviews.

The Scripture quotations contained herein are from the New Revised Standard Version of the Bible, copyright © 1989 by the Division of Christian Education of the National Council of Churches of Christ in the United States of America, and used by permission. All rights reserved.

Published by:

FpS

1175 Woods Crossing Rd., #5
Greenville, S.C. 29607
864-675-0540
www.fiction-addiction.com

ISBN: 978-1-945338-91-5

Library of Congress Control Number: 2017958340

Cover & Book Design by Vally Sharpe
Author Photograph © 2017 Jim Banks

Cover Photograph licensed from Shutterstock
Chapter ornament created by Freepik from www.flaticon.com

Printed in the United States of America.

To Jim

Contents

The Christmas Strawberry 1
A Season of Contrasts 21
Bursting with God-News 23
Advent 27
Is It Christmas Again? 29
Lesson 45
Pondering 47
How Many Tears Does It Take to Decorate a Christmas Tree? 51
Gray Christmas 53
If This Were Not a Special Time of Year 63
The Journey 65
The Gift 71
The Perfect Christmas 73
Be Not Afraid 83
Angelika's Christmas 89
Season's Greetings! 97
The Best Christmas Gift 99
Christmas Benediction 113

Acknowledgments 115
About the Author 117

The Christmas Strawberry

I have always loved Christmas. As a child, I sprayed aerosol snow on our windows, because with the outside temperature never going below 35 degrees, that was as close to a white Christmas as I could get. We put up our tree two Sundays before Christmas and decorated with all the ornaments that we'd collected or made through the years.

My favorite decoration was a glass strawberry that had been my grandmother's. Mama always placed it near the top of the tree so it would not get broken. We carefully draped silver "icicles" on every branch. When the big colored bulbs were plugged in, I swear I thought I was looking at heaven.

We had a nativity set with a cardboard stable. When you folded down the front, there stood all the Christmas characters glued into place. We put the stable under the tree and each day a few more presents appeared around it.

When I got married and was planning my first Christmas, Mama gave me the glass strawberry and the nativity set. Lee and I bought a kit to paint wooden ornaments for the tree. We had snowmen, Santa Clauses, bells, wooden soldiers, ballerinas, and drums. We filled in with ornaments that we bought at the Salvation Army store.

Lee and I argued about whether the tree needed icicles or not. I said that a tree was not complete without them. Lee said that his family had never used icicles because they looked tacky. We also argued about whether to have white lights or colored lights. Being the mature adults we were now that we were married, we compromised. He got his white lights and I got my icicles.

Our biggest disagreement, however, was over the nativity set. Lee was not raised in a church-going family. He didn't believe that Christmas was the birthday of Jesus. He said, "I don't want that stupid thing in my house, you hear?"

For him, Christmas was a time to decorate the house, spend time with friends, and get presents. Sometimes Christmas also meant, as he said, "sharing the spirit." So he'd go out drinking with his buddies.

I really didn't mind when Lee went out, because then I could pull out the nativity set and place it under the tree. I would put on Christmas music, pour myself some green Kool-Aid with a cherry in it to make a festive Christmas beverage, and celebrate in my own way. I hid the stable again before he came home.

When Linda was born, I looked forward to her first Christmas with all the excitement of a little kid. Even though she was only five months old, I wanted to begin building wonderful memories of Christmas for her so she could feel about the holiday like I did.

I made an ornament from a pattern that I found in one of the magazines at the check-out line at the grocery store. On the back, I wrote the date. I planned to make her an ornament every year until she left home to begin her own family. I bought a little camera so I could take pictures of her first special Christmas. I decided to put a photo of her in a small frame every year and hang it on the tree. I imagined her looking at a dozen of more of these small pictures with her own child and exclaiming, "This is what Mama looked like when I was your age." I also planned to create a scrapbook with just Christmas pictures so we could be reminded what we did each year, who came to visit us, and how we changed.

I bought Linda the cutest little elf outfit. She looked adorable in the green velour. Santa was going to bring her first baby doll and some soft blocks to play with.

Lee was not around much because he was out celebrating the Christmas spirits with his friends. I decorated the tree alone that year with Linda watching from her pallet on the floor. She was entranced with the lights and sparkly icicles. I told her the story about the strawberry ornament along with other stories I could remember about Christmases past. I began to tell her about the birth of Jesus as I placed the nativity set under the tree, but she fell asleep before I was finished. I lay down beside her on the floor and soon went to sleep myself.

I woke up with a start when Lee came home after a night with friends and kicked the nativity set across the room. "Please don't do that," I said, crying. "I'm sorry. I'll never put it out again. Please don't tear it up."

"I told you I don't want that kind of stuff in my home. Since it appears that I can't trust you to listen to me, I'll just put it in the garbage outside so I won't have to see it again."

With that he gave it another kick, picked it up, and stomped out to the garbage can and stuffed it in as far as he could. I unplugged the Christmas tree lights, put Linda in her crib, crawled into my bed, and turned my back to him while the tears leaked from my eyes.

After he left the house the next morning, I dug around in the garbage can to find the nativity set and assess the damage.

It looked bad. One side was bashed in. A wise man was missing his head but I found it rolling around in the back of the cardboard stable. The leg of Baby Jesus was gone and one shepherd was totally smashed into small pieces.

I took everything back into the house to see what I might salvage. I used silver duct tape to repair the holes to the stable itself. I figured the silver looked like the light of the star shining down. I was able to glue the wise man's head back on. The shepherd was destroyed, so I used a brown magic marker to color in the spot where he had been glued to the stable floor. Baby Jesus, however, was permanently wounded. I cried for him. He took the beating that Lee might have doled out to me. It hurt my heart.

After I finished my repairs, I hid the nativity set in the back of Linda's closet. I knew that Lee would never find it there. Every so often, I would pull it out when I knew that Lee would not be coming home. I sang lullabies to the injured baby and told Linda stories of Jesus as a baby and as a grown man.

Life went on. When Linda was two, Larry was born. He was a bouncy, happy child, whereas Linda seemed thoughtful and stared at things as if she were trying to solve the problems of the world. The children and I spent a lot of time together since Lee was rarely at home. An electrician, he traveled out of town to different work sites. As I said before, when he was in town, he often went out with his friends.

Despite all, Christmas continued to be my favorite holiday. With two children now, I had to scrimp even more so I could provide for them the kind of merry Christmas they deserved. I would have thought that Lee was making more money now that he had so much experience working, but if he was, I never saw it. He gave me the same amount of money for food and household items as he had when we first got married. No matter. I was creative and loved to visit thrift stores. No one could say that I did not take care of my kids properly!

Every time we went to the Salvation Army store, I looked for another nativity set. I rarely found a complete one, but occasionally I found some of the characters. I bought another shepherd. He was a little bigger than my other characters but that did not matter. I bought and added some sheep. One time, I even found a camel! My nativity set was really coming to life.

Occasionally, when I was feeling down, I pulled out the cardboard stable and talked with Jesus. I'd confess, "Jesus, I love you but sometimes I wonder if you love me. Life is so hard. Will you please give me a sign that you care about me?" I'd look at his poor little broken leg and know that he understood and was with me.

I also talked with Mary. I'd say, "Mary, teach me more about being a loving wife. I'm trying but it's really hard." Or I'd ask Joseph, "Joseph, you are a good man. How do you do it?" Sometimes I asked the wise men to bring me some spices, too, so I would feel special.

I hid all this from Lee. He was angry most of the time at home. I kept the children away from him because I was afraid that he might hurt them. He had hit me a time or two, but I deserved it because his dinner was cold or the children were crying and I couldn't get them to be quiet.

Just before Christmas, when Larry was three, I came home after spending the day with the children at the park, the Salvation Army store, and downtown looking at the pretty decorations, and found all our possessions on the sidewalk. I found a note posted on the front door saying that we had been evicted.

I could not understand what had happened. I knew this was a mistake so I went to our neighbor's house and knocked on the door. When she opened it, I said, "Hello, I'm not sure that you know me, but I live in the house across the street. Maybe you've seen me outside walking with my kids, Linda and Larry? Do you mind if I use your phone to call my landlord?"

She said, "Sure, honey. I've seen you in the neighborhood. My name's Anna. Is that all your stuff on the sidewalk over there?"

"Yes, and I don't know why it's out there. That's why I need to call my landlord."

"Come on in. I'll watch the kids while you make that call."

When my landlord's assistant finally answered, I told her who I was and that I was sure there had been a mistake.

"Hold on," she said. "Let me check."

I waited while I watched Anna entertain the children with some small toys she had in a drawer in the living room. The assistant finally came back on the line. "No, there's no mistake. Your rent has not been paid for the last three months."

"That can't be right. My husband pays every month."

"Well, he may, but the money has not come to *our* office."

I hung up the phone in horrified amazement. I pulled the children close as if to protect them from the shocking news I'd just received.

Anna asked, "Is everything okay?" I burst into tears and told her what had happened. Sweet angel that she was, she said, "I'll watch the kids. You go out and see what you can save from that pile of stuff on the sidewalk."

That shocked me into action. I had to act quickly. Everything I owned was outside. If I didn't hurry, people would be like vultures picking through my things. I focused on gathering the children's clothes and favorite toys. I found some of my clothes and a few pots and pans. However, it wasn't long before other people were there trying to find things to sell for food or drugs. Even though I screamed at them to go away, they kept coming until before long, only garbage that no one wanted was left.

Anna and I had never really known each other even though we'd been neighbors for a while. Her children were grown and she worked. But she reached out to me and told me that the kids and I could stay with her until after Christmas.

I accepted her offer, because I needed to stay close so when Lee came home, I could give him what for!

But Lee never came back.

To this day, I have not actually seen him. He had a man track me down and give me divorce papers to sign, but that's the only thing I ever heard from him.

Anna, dear sweet Anna, tried her best to help the children have a decent Christmas that year. She pulled out toys that she'd saved from her own kids. She had a tree covered in shiny purple and gold balls. But she didn't use icicles and she had white lights.

I hurt deep inside when I automatically looked to the top of the tree for grandma's glass strawberry and it wasn't there. And, there was no nativity set.

I wondered who Anna talked to if she didn't have Mary and Jesus and Joseph and the wise men and the shepherds. I desperately wanted to talk with Joseph so he could tell me how to get Lee to come back and be a good husband and father.

On Christmas Eve, I still told the children the story of Christmas and about God's love for us. I told them, "Anna is an angel just like the angels of the story. The angel told the shepherds to be not afraid and that's what Anna has told us. Don't be afraid!" The children's eyes got huge.

Anna blushed and said, "Don't go telling those children such foolishness."

I wanted the children to have a good memory of Christmas and not associate this wonderful holiday with the tragedy that had happened to us. I think Anna and I succeeded for the most part.

Christmas evening after my children were in bed and Anna's grown kids had left, Anna and I sat in the living room and stared at the Christmas tree. She made me a cup of tea that she kept for special occasions. When she had settled into the sofa with her legs pulled up under her and I was sitting in a chair with comfy cushions, she asked, "What are you going to do now?"

I looked at her for a long time before speaking. "I don't know."

"Can you go back home to your mother's?"

I thought for a minute and said, "I don't think so. Anyway, I'd rather make it on my own."

"Well, you can stay here until New Year's. After that you will have to leave."

I nodded my head. "I understand. Thanks for all you've already done for us."

The next day I got busy calling agencies to ask about shelters where we might live until I could get stable income. I asked about jobs and job programs. It was a long and disappointing process, but eventually, I found a place where we could live as long as I participated in a job training program.

The lady on the phone explained: "You will have to come to the office to sign up. I can give you an appointment for next Tuesday at 2:30. Bring identification papers for you and your children."

Fortunately, I had always kept that kind of important information in my pocketbook, so I had what I needed. Thank you, Jesus, that the documents had not been thrown in the pile on the side of the road.

Anna helped me get to the appointment. I found out that I was approved for the program, but that I'd have to wait for two months until the next cycle began.

Two months? What were the children and I supposed to do in the meantime? I had no choice but to call my mother and ask her if we could stay with her. She didn't want to let us come, but I told her about the program that we were going to be in and I promised we'd be gone at the end of two months. She reluctantly agreed.

I enrolled Linda into school as soon as we moved, but I wasn't sure what I could do with Larry. Ma said, "Just bring him with us." I wasn't sure at first what she meant. I guess she saw the confusion on my face. "As long as you are living with me," she said, "you can help me with my housecleaning jobs. Larry can come along if he can be quiet."

So, that's what we did.

Finally, the day came when we could move into the shelter. The program would allow us to stay for twelve months. As we settled into our room and I began my job training, it seemed that life improved greatly.

My Christmas miracle came a little late that year, but from having all our things being put on the sidewalk just before Christmas to being taken in by Anna and then receiving a safe shelter to live in with my kids just a few months later with the opportunity to learn a job felt like having the wise men show up and give me all three of their wonderful gifts at one time.

Our year in the training program was wonderful. The kids settled down since they were no longer living in fear of what their father might do whenever he showed up. They enjoyed the rhythm and schedule of the program. Linda liked her school and Larry thrived in the preschool program that a church provided.

I was thrilled when I realized that I was smart. I learned all kinds of computer programs to prepare me to be an office assistant. After about six months, I started working at various companies to learn on-the-job things. I made friends and felt good about myself.

In early December, I realized that Christmas was going to be different this year. The staff and area churches tried to make us feel loved and cared for during the holiday. They decorated everywhere and different groups brought in refreshments as well as presents for the children. I was happy for Linda and Larry, but it made me feel bad that others were providing for my kids what I could not. I knew that people just wanted to make this time special for us and let us know that someone cared and loved us. We *did* know that people could be good.

However, I often woke up in the night remembering my own tree with its glass strawberry, icicles, and nativity set. The big tree in the main living room, as beautiful as it was, did not have the same meaning for me as our own little trees in the past did.

I especially missed my nativity set. Even though the facility had a gorgeous stable with all the characters (none of them were missing any parts), I never felt like talking with any of them. Mary was just a beautiful figurine. Joseph was a stiff, cool object. Baby Jesus was a beautiful baby but he was not wounded.

How could he relate to my life and what I and my children had been through? That Mary, Joseph, and Baby couldn't. They did not have life like my own nativity set did.

On Christmas morning that year, the children in the shelter received more presents. Santa brought all the girls dolls and the boys cars. Every child also got a game and a hand-knitted cap.

All of us mothers received sweet smelling soaps, a pair of warm socks, a bottle of nail polish, and a Bible. Our meal together that day had all the usual Christmas foods: turkey, sweet potato casserole, dressing, congealed fruit salad, and Christmas cookies.

I know I should not complain, but when I slipped into bed that night, I still felt a big hole inside where the warmth of Christmas should have been. However, when both of my children crawled into my bed to snuggle and whisper how much they loved Christmas, I pushed that empty feeling down. I was already so richly blessed. What was wrong with me?

That night I had a dream. My baby Jesus, the one with the broken leg, came to me. He said, "Fear not."

That's all I remember, but wow…that was amazing.

During the last couple of months in the program, the staff helped me find a job and a place for us to live. Some lovely church ladies met with me to find out what kinds of furniture and household items I might need. Then they asked me to meet with their group and tell them my story.

Since they had been so kind to me, I agreed, even though I was scared. After I finished telling them what had happened, they said they had a surprise for me.

They opened a door to another room filled with almost everything I had told them I needed. A few days later, they and their husbands helped me move into my own home. They said that they would like to continue to be my friends and help me when I needed it. They promised that they would mostly just be my friends, but if I wanted some guidance or helpful hints about dealing with a situation, they'd be there. They invited me and the kids to come to their church, but made it clear that they'd be my "sisters-in-Christ" whether we worshiped there or not. (Of course, we did.)

When the kids and I left the program that had been our life for the last twelve months, we were both sad and excited. We were sad to leave such wonderful people but were excited to be in our own place.

Our apartment was in the same neighborhood as the program, so Linda did not have to change schools. The church pre-school program where Larry went said they loved him so much that they wanted him to continue staying there so I could work without having to worry about him.

Fortunately, I could catch the bus to get to my job. For the first time in my life, I worked with people who respected me and valued my contribution. I studied what the other women wore to work and then shopped weekly at the Salvation Army store to find outfits that looked like theirs. I enjoyed the responsibility of my job and the opportunity to earn a basic salary so I could take care of my children on my own.

One day I was shopping and, as always, I looked in the housewares section. I liked looking for decorative items that could make our apartment feel even more like home. Sometimes I found a picture to hang on the wall. Many times I bought a pretty glass or plate for our table. I bought a toaster and a blender there. On this day, though, I was not looking for anything in particular.

Even though it was only September, they were already putting out Christmas decorations that people had donated. Out of habit, I poked through the plastic bin that a worker had just brought in from the warehouse. I looked through the misshaped poinsettias, the tangled lights, and the ugly plastic Christmas balls. I had just about moved on to look at the kids' toys when I noticed a half-full box of icicles. I got so excited that I kept digging deeper and deeper in the box.

And then I saw it! There was my grandmother's glass strawberry ornament! It was missing its hanger loop and had a small chip in the side but it was THE strawberry.

I forgot about looking for anything else. I took the strawberry and icicles to the cash register, gave the clerk my dollar for the two items, and floated home.

I decided not to tell the children what I had found. That would be part of their Christmas surprise. After they went to bed, I worked on the strawberry to fashion a ribbon hanger for it. Every time I held the beautiful red glass in my hand, I felt like I was holding my grandma's hand. When I think about it, I think it was the other way around. She was holding mine.

As Christmas got closer and closer, I began planning our celebration. I signed the children up to be in the Christmas pageant at our church. Linda was going to be a shepherdess and Larry was a sheep. I asked my sisters-in-Christ if they knew how to make the costumes that Linda and Larry needed.

They said, "Don't worry. You just focus on your job and getting presents for your kids. We'll take care of the costumes." I was very grateful for their help.

When I saw the kids all dressed up, they looked so cute I thought I would burst with pride. They were excited about being in the pageant and asked me to tell them the Christmas story over and over because they wanted to get their parts exactly right.

I loved telling them about Mary, Joseph, the baby Jesus, the shepherds, wise men, and angels. Now that they were bigger, I could tell them about God's love for us and remind them how God had taken such good care of us. I told them how God had given us Anna when we had no home to go to. I told them how the people in the program and the nice church people had been God's angels to us. And I told them the people where I worked were certainly wise and a gift from God.

"And the shepherds?" they asked. "Who are the shepherds?"

I said, "Well, the shepherds and sheep were the most important of all. The sisters-in-Christ are our shepherds as they watch over us in the church. We are their sheep and they are careful to make sure that nothing will harm us again."

On one occasion, I told Linda and Larry about our old nativity set. I explained how Baby Jesus had lost a leg in an accident when the stable got dropped. My eyes watered up a bit when I told them how much I'd loved that Baby Jesus and his missing leg because as a grown up, Jesus had loved us. He took care of us even when he was hurt just like my Baby Jesus.

As I wiped my eyes, claiming that I'd been peeling onions, I told them: "God is still with us, even though I no longer have the nativity set. Every time I look at your faces, I see the love of God shining through your beautiful eyes. Every time one of you gives me a kiss, I know that Jesus is right here with us. Every time the happiness of our lives bubbles up so that we laugh out loud, the spirit of God is here—loving us, guiding us, and taking care of us."

Linda and Larry looked at me with expressions of wonderment that lasted a few seconds until Larry got up to do whatever little boys do when they get bored with the conversation. Linda, however, remained quiet as she helped me prepare our supper.

The children loved going to the rehearsals for the Christmas pageant. They made even more friends. One of the girls, Julie, a daughter of a sister-in-Christ, invited Linda to her house to spend the night. I was pleased to see that Linda was making friends and finally having what I would call a "normal" childhood. That also gave Larry and me time alone together.

After the first sleepover, Linda came home excited about what she and Julie had done and the fun she'd had. She asked if she could go home with Julie after church on Sunday, and I said, "Sure."

After that, Linda began spending so much time at her new friend's house that I started to get my feelings hurt. I thought that she no longer wanted to be with me—that she was embarrassed by me. I was beginning to resent the Christmas pageant and what it was doing to my relationship with my daughter.

The day of the pageant finally arrived. I prepared to help Linda put on her costume at home, but she said, "No thanks. I'm dressing at Julie's house." I tried not to let my disappointment show, but I think Linda knew that I was not happy.

"Mom," she said, "thanks for bringing us to this church. I love it and I love you. I'll see you after the pageant." With that, she ran off to get in Julie's mother's car that was waiting out front.

As I turned around, I saw Larry watching me closely. I pasted on a smile and said, "Come on, Mr. Sheep. Let's get you ready." He brightened up when he looked at the sheep staring back at him in the mirror. He loved the stares that he got as we rode the bus to church.

I guided Larry to where the other sheep were gathering and then went to find a seat. I could feel the excitement in the air. Everyone was thrilled to watch their children.

The entire audience waited to see what hilarious mishap would occur this year. I had already heard stories of the innkeeper who had once announced to Mary and Joseph, "Come on in. There's plenty of room" and about the angel who felt faint and whispered loud enough for everyone to hear, "Get this *#&* halo off my head before I puke."

The lights dimmed and I watched enrapt as the children went through the familiar words. I felt my heart warm just as it had when I placed that cardboard nativity set under my tree. I thought I would burst with pride when I saw my children handle their parts with the right mixture of solemnness and joy.

When the children finished, all of us parents stood up and clapped and clapped. Some dads whistled. The children's smiles could have lit up New York City as they beamed with pride.

The director came onto the stage and thanked the children. Then she asked everyone to please sit back down. We glanced around the room to see what else might be happening. Everyone seemed as puzzled as I was.

Once again, the lights dimmed. The spotlight shone only on the director.

"This year," she said, "we have a special addition to our pageant. What you have just witnessed is your beautiful children bringing to life the nativity story. Even though they get to see the characters in the nativity sets that you display at home, this pageant allows them to put flesh onto those lifeless characters.

"However, sometimes those nativity sets in your homes seem to have lives of their own even though Mary, Joseph, the baby and all the other characters are made of wood, clay, resin, metal, glass, or cloth.

"On rare occasions, the members of the holy family and the supporting cast in your stables brim full of love and grace and joy. Tonight, I want to share one such nativity set with you."

The director looked at my daughter, who was standing offstage. "Linda, will you please roll out that table? Thank you."

I watched Linda roll out a cart with a wooden box on it. Then she took a shepherd from the box.

The director smiled. "Linda, tell us about this shepherd and all the other characters."

Linda looked out in the audience at me. "My friend Julie and I made them out of sticks, glue, wire, and bits of cloth. Julie's mom helped, but mostly we did it ourselves." I was frozen in my seat.

Then Linda held up Baby Jesus.

The director pretended to look more closely at the baby. "It looks like you missed something here," she said. "This baby is missing a leg."

Linda shook her head. "No, we planned it that way. You see, Jesus was wounded even as a baby so that he could love us in the mighty way that he does. My mom taught me about God's grace. That's why I made this nativity set for her."

I could no longer control my tears. I ran to the stage and hugged Linda. People surrounded us, laughing and crying at the same time.

When things calmed down a bit, we all went to the fellowship hall for punch and Christmas cookies. And when we were all done, Julie and her mother, my sister-in-Christ, drove Linda, Larry, and me home with the most beautiful nativity set I had ever seen—one I would treasure for the rest of my life.

A Season of Contrasts

This time of year is full of contrasts:
Darkness of winter…light of Christmas
Excess of the celebration…inadequacy of resources to celebrate
Expressions of love and joy…desperation of depression and loneliness
Hope of the birth of a baby…fear of what will happen to all children
Special traditions…inability to build traditions
Expectations of gifts…despair of having anything
Anticipation of time spent with family…anxiety of family dynamics
The contrasts affect us all.
Some of us live more on one side
Than the other.
When we reach out across the contrast,
All our lives are enriched.

Bursting with God-News

When Mary was pregnant with the baby Jesus, she went to visit her cousin Elizabeth. As soon as Mary greeted her relative, Elizabeth felt her own baby move within her womb. Both women rejoiced in the experience they were sharing—Elizabeth blessed her cousin and Mary burst into song.

Mary was fortunate that she had someone like Elizabeth in her life. Her cousin was able to confirm what was in Mary's inmost heart—that Mary was the mother of the Lord.

She knew on a deep level what God was calling her to do but may have been a bit afraid to fully embrace that call. She may have tried to talk herself out of what was happening within her body and yet, probably felt foolish even to be thinking that way. Morning sickness likely did not help. In the middle of the night when she couldn't sleep, Mary may have thought of all the reasons she could not possibly be the person to pursue the dream God had planted in her innermost being. She may have yearned for someone to help her take that next challenging step.

Now that she had arrived in the hill country and been blessed by Elizabeth, Mary was happy. She sang that she was bursting with God-news. She danced around Elizabeth's kitchen and rejoiced in what God was doing. She even dreamed that people would talk about her as being the mother of the long-awaited Messiah. She sang of her love for God and God's love for her. She was an exuberant teenage girl with a wonderful, magnificent miracle happening within her.

Even so, why was she so happy? She was lowly. She was already engaged to Joseph. She had never borne a child. She was not learned in the Scriptures. Why in the world would God choose someone such as she to be the mother of God's son? It made no sense. It was the craziest thing that could have happened. To think that God would choose to come into the world the way all humans did—through childbirth as a baby—vulnerable, immature, and with wet swaddling cloths! And yet that is the very thing God said would happen.

God's choosing to come into the world as the baby of a peasant family was as ridiculous as the hungry being fed and the powerful being toppled. In her own life, Mary was experiencing a complete upending of the natural order, of the way things should be. She was literally experiencing in her body a reversal of the general expectations of the world.

These kinds of things were not supposed to happen, and especially not to someone who had no position, no authority, and no prestige. When the realization of all this hit her, what else could she have done except sing and dance? Because of her own experience, Mary announced in her song that God had also scattered those who are proud, knocked tyrants off their high horse, put humble people in places of power, filled the hungry with good things, and sent the rich away empty.

Mary saw those very things happening in her own life.

Mary sang of her experience of God's activity. She lifted up in joy what she already knew: God values humble folks and hungry people and does not place much value on powerful or rich people. She sang about a wonderful, magnificent, astounding personal relationship with the Lord God Almighty.

Her song was about the pure, unadulterated, gleeful joy that happens in God's world—where everyone has what he or she needs and where society has a healthy balance to it. Mary knew that God was already bringing these things to reality. What good news for those who suffer and are heavy-laden! God is giving them rest and will continue to give them rest. What good news for those without power! God has, is, and will give them power.

Mary did not *decide* to become the mother of God's son. She just was...by God's actions. What else could Mary and Elizabeth do but join hands and circle around and around in the room that was now filled with laughter?

And so, Mary sang: "My soul magnifies the Lord, and my spirit rejoices in God my savior, for he has looked with favor on the lowliness of his servant. Surely, from now on all generations will call me blessed; for the Mighty One has done great things for me, and holy is his name. His mercy is for those who fear him from generation to generation. He has shown strength with his arm; he has scattered the proud in the thoughts of their hearts. He has brought down the powerful from their thrones, and lifted up the lowly; he has filled the hungry with good things, and sent the rich away empty. He has helped his servant Israel, in remembrance of his mercy, according to the promise he made to our ancestors, to Abraham and to his descendants forever" (Luke 1: 47-55).

Advent

Advent is…

The time of waiting:
Waiting in the dark
Waiting with the unknown
Waiting for the grief to pass
Waiting for the old to loosen its hold
Waiting for the new to begin
Waiting with uncertainty
Waiting with impatience
Waiting with hope
Waiting without hope
Waiting in blindness
Waiting…waiting…waiting

I'm not a good wait…er.
Lord, Jesus, come quickly.

Author's note: Advent is the Christian church season that is celebrated for four Sundays prior to Christmas. Its themes are often hope, joy, love, and peace. It is a time of anticipating the birth of the Savior and of the fullness of time in God's love.

Is It Christmas Again?

On July 5, I dragged myself out of bed. I had not slept well because of all the firecrackers and other noisy incendiary devices that were set off by uncaring people all night long. Why in the world July 4 calls out all the crazy nuts who love to dally with risky, arson-causing noisemakers, I'll never know. And if I see another person wearing red, white, and blue, especially with stars and stripes somewhere on their person, I'll scream.

I looked in the mirror. The face I saw was not the face that I expected. This face had dark circles under the eyes with wrinkles on either side. The lips were thin with huge parentheses running on either side from the mouth to the nose. The skin was blotchy. And the hair? Oh, my! It looked like the fur of a cat caught in a bad rainstorm. Who was this person looking at me?

Unfortunately, I knew that the image had to be mine. No one else lived with me. I'd been single now longer than I was single before I got married. Just one more thing to celebrate.

Yippee!

Since I didn't have to work because of the long holiday weekend, I was planning to go out for a cup of coffee and then to a craft store to see if I might get inspired to be creative. Making something fun or beautiful sometimes helped pull me out of the dreary room in my head, one where I spent too much time. I hoped that just the effort of getting dressed and out of my apartment would improve my attitude.

I enjoyed sitting in the café watching people come and go. While I sipped my double latte, I made up stories of the people waiting at the counter or sitting at the tables. That woman in the corner had just realized she was getting older and that no one wanted her anymore. The young couple who looked as if they'd just gotten out of bed and threw on the first thing they found lying on the floor had spent a wild night making love. By the end of the month, they'd each have moved on to someone else. That man, the scruffy one, lost everything he had due to his drinking. Now he was trying to be sober, but it was a struggle.

Then I realized that even the stories I was making up were depressing. I finished my coffee and headed to the craft store.

What a dismal experience! Here I was with the echoes of fireworks still buzzing in my ears and Halloween and fall decorations were already out. It was ninety-one degrees outside, after all! Rush, rush, rush. No wonder I felt tired all the time.

Oh, no. Just two aisles away from the leaves, pumpkins, scarecrows, and witches, clerks were stocking Christmas ornaments and greenery. This felt almost sacrilegious! I remember when I used to love to look at Christmas ornaments and plan how I would change some of my over-the-top Christmas décor. Now, in July, everything just looked trashy and cheap. What do all these themed ornaments have to do with Christmas, anyway? Cowboys? Mini-chandeliers with Victorian feather fans? What? Tacky, tacky, tacky!

On to the craft section. I looked at the yarns, but I'd already knitted at least one scarf for everyone I knew. I wandered over to the cross-stitch section. I loved looking at the colors of thread and the new kinds of fabric. I especially enjoyed looking at the pattern books, but my impaired eyesight made needlework harder and less pleasurable. And, once again, everyone already had at least one cross-stitched item from me.

Scrapbooking? I liked the different papers but thought the concept of putting one picture on a page with lots of cutesy things around it was wasteful. Quilting? I loved touching the fabrics but never could convince myself to spend the time to learn how to make a quilt in the old-fashioned way with piecing and appliqué—using small, tiny, neat stitches. I didn't have a group of friends to hang out with who could participate in a quilting bee like those I'd read about.

Up and down the aisles I wandered. I briefly looked at sewing patterns but the last time I tried to make something for me, it didn't fit. The entire endeavor was a waste of time.

I looked at the home décor items and considered purchasing a new vase to keep flowers in but then I wondered who would provide the flowers to go into the vase? My kids usually sent flowers once a year on Mother's Day. I might remember... maybe once a month or so...to pick up flowers at the grocery store. Otherwise the vase would just sit on the table taking up precious space and collecting dust.

I finally decided to get a couple of easy kits to make some Christmas ornaments. I could always give them to co-workers or my neighbors. Beginning to work on Christmas things in July went against everything I felt about Christmas, but I had to find something creative to do! The kits seemed easy and if the final result looked like the picture, I'd be pleased with my efforts.

I went back home, threw the craft store bag on a chair in my bedroom, and took a nap. Because people didn't shoot off fireworks in the middle of the day, I could sleep. I muddled through the weekend until Monday when I went back to work.

I made it through Halloween with no difficulty. I managed to drink my coffee without gagging too much when served by a barista dressed like a witch. Only one or two people dressed up at my workplace. Really, the head of the human relations department dressed as a clown? How ironic is that? I cut off all the lights in my apartment and turned off my outside light. No little urchins stopped at my door.

The problem with Halloween, however, is that the next day is the first day of November and, on that day, the Christmas machine moves into high gear. Everywhere there is Christmas music. All the stores are decorated. Television bombards us with Christmas commercials. The after-Thanksgiving sales begin weeks *before* Thanksgiving so that when the holiday comes, everything is usually picked over. Besides, people don't stay home after their big Thanksgiving meals with, as they say, friends and loved ones, because the stores are now open on Thanksgiving to sell, sell, sell the latest gadget, the newest toy, and the junkiest junk.

Because all our grown kids had other plans for the Thanksgiving holiday and lived several hours away, some friends from work and I had planned to celebrate together. However, I came down with the flu and had to cancel. I was alone… and sick. It was just as well—I couldn't think of much to be thankful for anyway.

When I finally felt strong enough to be able to talk on the phone (I wanted to hear my kids' voices rather than send them a text or an e-mail message), I called each of them. I wanted to make sure of our Christmas plans.

I called my son first. "Did you have a good Thanksgiving? Oh, good. I'm glad that you and your friends enjoyed being together. How are the kids? Good. Are they looking forward to the Christmas break? Yeah? Well, that's what I wanted to talk with you about. I wanted to know where and when we are going to get together to celebrate Christmas.

"Oh? Disney World? Well, of course, the kids are a perfect age for that. When are you leaving? Oh. Well, maybe we can get together early in the New Year.

"Sure, sure. I'll spend Christmas with your sister and her husband. Don't you worry about me. You all just have a wonderful time. We'll talk again before you go, of course. I'll get the kids' presents together and put them in the mail or we'll just have Christmas whenever we get together next. Christmas doesn't *have* to be celebrated on December 25, does it? I love you and miss you. Give the kids a big hug and kiss from me. Goodbye."

I fixed myself a cup of peppermint tea to help calm my stomach before I called my daughter.

"Hello, sweetie. How was Thanksgiving? Yeah, it's too bad that you had to work the day after. That didn't feel much like a holiday, did it? "What did you do on Thanksgiving Day? You went to a cafeteria? How was that? Me?

"Well, some friends from work and I had plans to get together but…What? I called you just as you were about to call me? That's nice. What did you want to tell me?

"Oh, I see. A Christmas cruise for just the two of you. Yes, I can see how important that is when you both have been working so hard. I completely understand. You two go and have a good time. Don't you worry about me. I'll be fine. I love you, too. Goodbye."

Christmas was coming…and I was going to be alone.

Everywhere I turned people seemed to be filled with Christmas cheer. I watched the unending array of Christmas movies until I was so overwhelmed by the happy endings that I just couldn't take it anymore. I pulled out the Christmas ornament kits that I'd bought back in July, but I still couldn't get started with the project. I shuffled through the days. When co-workers mentioned that I seemed a little down, I told them I was still trying to get over the flu bug that I had at Thanksgiving.

During lunch breaks, people began sharing their Christmas plans. I tried to act interested but sometimes simply had to excuse myself with the explanation that I had some calls I needed to make or a report I had to complete. Nobody asked if I had any special plans.

I had pulled out a couple of boxes of my Christmas decorations, but they still sat exactly where I left them in the hall. I just couldn't get into the Christmas spirit. Even going to church was depressing. Everywhere preparations for the "Big Event" were happening. The choir was singing their usual glorious music. The huge Christmas tree in the worship space was complete with its white and gold ornaments. Poinsettias were everywhere. Church ladies with red aprons served special cookies after worship. The television screens around the church routinely announced all the additional services and holiday get-togethers. All of this reinforced my loneliness.

At the end of the last day of work before the holiday, I went home and took off my coat. I didn't even turn on the light. I thought about my children and grandchildren and their fun holiday plans. I wondered if they'd even think about me.

At church that Sunday, people chirped "Merry Christmas," but that was all the notice I received. The barista wore a Santa hat and asked if I'd like some cinnamon sprinkled in my coffee for holiday cheer. Although I felt no cheer, I said, "Sure."

I opened a can of soup and turned on the radio only to be bombarded by awful Christmas music. Whatever happened to *White Christmas* or *Silver Bells*? I think a couple of musicians may have sung those tunes but by the time they were finished with all their "extra touches," I hardly recognized them. I finally turned the noise off.

I sat down and realized that no one cared whether I was here or not. Not my children or grandchildren, not my co-workers, not my church members, and probably not even my barista. I stared into the dark space until I decided I'd go to bed, even though it was a couple of hours before I normally turned in. I didn't shower as I usually do or put on pajamas.

I went into the bathroom, brushed my teeth, looked into the mirror and once again saw that stranger looking back at me. No wonder nobody else noticed me. I hardly recognized myself.

I opened the medicine cabinet and took out the bottle of sleeping pills. I rarely took the prescription but tonight I figured that I needed help sleeping. I noticed that the bottle was almost full. I took a second pill, reasoning that I didn't want to chance flopping around all night wide awake and brooding.

And then I swallowed another. And another. I took the entire bottle and lay down on my bed.

When I woke up, I was sitting in a chair with beautiful blown-glass Christmas balls hanging all around me at eye level and above and below me. I was horrified to know that I was not dressed appropriately for this place. I looked down to try to smooth out my wrinkled clothes and saw, to my great surprise, that I was wearing a dress made of something that looked like butterfly wings laced with flecks of sparkly mica. My hands were beautiful—there were no wrinkles or age spots. I could see up close and far away with no vision problems. I settled into this comfortable chair, leaned my head back, and closed my eyes. This experience was so pleasant that I wanted to savor it.

Then I heard bells getting louder and louder. These bells

had a sound that I struggle to explain. They sounded a bit like pealing church bells but then at other times, they sounded like jingle bells. As the intriguing sounds got stronger, I realized that they were coming closer to me. When I opened my eyes, I could not see anyone carrying them, however. Then the beautiful tinkling stopped.

I sat, fully relaxed, with no anxiety. This event was beyond anything I had ever experienced but I felt no fear. I waited. I breathed…deeply. I felt refreshed and…what? I felt cherished. I felt, yes, that was it, I felt cherished. I had not felt that way in a long time.

Then, a being came to me. At first, I could not discern whether this being was human or animal. I knew that whatever, whoever, it was would cause me no harm. In what seemed to be just a few minutes, the being became recognizable to me as a human kind of shape but with wings. It…she…he…reminded me of the books I pored over as a child. I had loved studying the pictures of angels and fairies. For lack of any other way to describe this magnificent creature, I'll call it an angel.

I looked into the angel's face and saw such powerful love there shining at me, I could not maintain eye contact. I looked down. The angel spoke. "My dear child, you have been so lonely and despondent."

I replied, "Oh, no. I've just been going through a rough patch. But things will get better."

The angel would not let me continue to delude myself. "You believe that your life has no meaning, that if you left the earth, no one would care."

I stared at her. How could she know? I looked again into that face, those eyes. I nodded *yes*.

"Now that you are here, you can listen to what we have to say."

Another angel appeared and pulled out a paper rolled up like a scroll, dramatically took off the ribbon around it, unrolled it and read: "Thanks. You're a real Godsend…and God sends nothing but the best. You have made these moments together the best!"

I was puzzled. Noting this, the angel explained, "This came to us as a prayer. We believe that people meant to let you know special things but forgot to put them in writing for you. They send them to us as thoughts or prayers. We wanted to share with you what the woman you chat with sometimes when you are sitting in the park intended to say to you in person."

Another angel appeared and repeated the process. This time the angel read: "I want to say thank you for meeting with me to talk about your life experiences. Although my desire to meet you was prompted by a class assignment, I left the meeting feeling encouraged and inspired. I learned a lot. I really appreciate your willingness to sit down with me and talk about your experiences. It's nice to be reassured that if I follow my instincts and the path that is laid out for me, I will end up where I am supposed to be. It was great to hear the story of your journey. Thank you for candidly sharing with me your experience."

Once again, I had no idea who might have "sent" this message. The angel informed me that this was from an intern my company hosted for a week several years ago. I remembered nothing of the conversation or the face of the intern.

Another scroll was unrolled. It said, "You have helped

me grow. Thank you for your prayers, your support, and your encouragement."

I shook my head with wonder. Who could have said such a thing? The angel told me this message had arrived about five years ago from a co-worker of mine who was new to the company. I was astounded. This person still worked where I did, but I had no idea of the impact I had had on her.

Yet another angel appeared. He said his message came from a member of my church after I'd led a Sunday school class about hunger. "Your talk in Church School last Sunday was just perfect," he read. "You have a gift of enthusiasm, tempered with a sense of warmth for the audience. The combination makes people want to listen to you for they feel you are sincere in your message. I have always thought that God put you where you are so your particular character would be used best. You bring needed changes in a caring way."

I realized that tears were streaming down my face. I had thought no one cared about me.

At this point, another angel came in with a basket full of scrolls. She pulled one out and read, "My husband and I were talking the other day about community and heroes. He told me that you are one of his—specifically because you do what you do and you are who you are. I would ditto his sentiment and also say that we are grateful and better people for knowing you."

All I could do was shake my head when the angel told me that they had received this message from a former neighbor of mine. I remembered speaking to them and occasionally sharing a meal with them or watching their little girl when they went out on a date night. I never, however, thought that I what I did was anything special.

The angel pulled several more scrolls out of the basket. "And these are from your family," he said.

"Thank you, Mom, because you helped make growing up bearable." "It's so tough being perfect. My guess is that I got it from you." I was stunned.

The angel said, "There are many, many more scrolls that we could share with you about how your life has impacted others, but our time with you is running short. We'll end our time together by reading this message that came to us from your parents when you were eight years old."

It said, "We are grateful for the generosity of yourself in unselfish ways of love and caring—not only to family—but to the neighborhood—and to many others with no family."

All I could do was try to catch my breath and sit in wonder. How did I not know? Or had I known once upon a time and forgotten when I began to feel sorry for myself?

I felt totally drained because of the powerful emotions I'd experienced as I sat in that wonderful place hearing the melodious words of the luminous, caring, and wise angels. I closed my eyes and cherished the many words that had been shared.

Then, suddenly, all the peace and serenity were jerked away. People were shouting at me. Painful needles were being put into my body. Glaring lights scared me. Clanging bells surrounded me. I heard a lot of people talking but not in the soothing tones of the beautiful angels who had read me the touching messages. What was happening?

I began crying tears—not of joy but of terror. I heard a horrible noise and realized that it was coming from me. I slowly opened my eyes and saw all kinds of people in white and green moving around the room. Finally, my eyes focused on one person who was leaning against my bed with fear in her face. That face belonged to my daughter.

What happened? What was going on? Why was my daughter here? I searched her face for answers. I tried to speak but had something in my mouth and throat and couldn't say anything.

"Mom, don't try to talk," said my daughter. "Do you know where you are?"

I moved my eyes side to side as if shaking my head *no*, and she said, "You are in the hospital." I scrunched my eyes in puzzlement.

She took a deep breath. "Mom, you took an overdose of sleeping pills. I kept trying to call you all evening to tell you to pack your bag because my brother and I had planned a trip for you with our families as a big surprise for Christmas. I was going to pick you up this morning and whisk you away.

"When I couldn't get an answer, I got scared and called the apartment manager who found you. He called an ambulance and then me.

"Mom, you just about died. In fact, at one point, they thought you *had* died."

I closed my eyes again. I could not take in what my daughter was telling me. I took an overdose of sleeping pills? My family had planned a big Christmas surprise for me? What about the beautiful place with the wonderful messages for me?

I settled back into my pillow and tuned out everything that was happening around me. I dosed off with the realization that my daughter was sitting beside my bed holding my hand.

The next day, December 23, my daughter took me back to my apartment. When we opened the door, I was glad that I was leaning on my daughter's arm. There were my son and his wife, both the grandchildren, and my daughter's husband. My apartment was fully decorated for Christmas. I could not speak, in part because my throat was still very sore from the tubes pushed down it in the hospital, but also because I was in shock.

My first thought was, *I've cost them a pile of money. My grandchildren were going to Disney World and my daughter was going on a cruise.* As soon as I sat down on the sofa, I said, "I'm so sorry, so, so, sorry."

They all looked genuinely puzzled. My son said, "Mom, why are *you* sorry? We're the ones who are sorry. We let you think that you were going to be all alone on Christmas. We all know how special this time of the year is for you and we acted as if we did not care. No, *we* are sorry." He looked around at everyone and they all nodded their heads, even the children.

I started crying again. "No, my stupid act cost you your trip to Disney World with the kids," and I looked at my daughter's husband. "And the cruise for the two of you was to be a special time because you both work so hard and don't have time for each other."

"Mom, you don't get it," said my daughter. "The Disney World trip and the cruise were ruses. The kids were not going to Disney World and we were not going on a cruise. We planned a surprise trip for all of us—including you—to the mountains. We've rented a house with enough room for everyone."

I was perplexed.

She continued. "The good news is that we still have the house. We've been able to delay our arrival by a couple of days. We're leaving tomorrow morning, Christmas Eve…all of us…so we can be together as a family to celebrate Jesus's birth with you."

I was speechless. One of my grandchildren crawled into my lap, hugged my neck hard, planted a big wet kiss on my cheek, and said, "I love you, Grandma. I want to spend Christmas with you and not some dressed-up characters like scary animals or princesses."

"You do so much for other people," said my daughter-in-law. "No one really thanks you for all you do for us and everyone. We wanted to do this special thing to show you how much we love you."

My son sat down beside me, his eyes filled with tears. "Mom, I don't want to think about a world without you."

I bit my lip to try to stop my own tears from flowing again and rose up from the sofa. "Enough! I've got packing to do!"

Tomorrow, we would celebrate together the most wonderful Christmas gift of all…love!

Lesson

As I was walking in the country
One crisp, bright winter day
I saw a lone tree
Pointing upwards with majesty.
Its solitude touched my deep ache
Of human living…yearning.
And then I saw two trees
Leaning to each other.
And that moment I knew…
That only together can we survive
Can we care
Can we celebrate
The wonder of this special time of year.

Pondering

"But Mary treasured all these words and pondered them in her heart."
~ Luke 2:19 ~

"Ponder" is an interesting word, not used much in today's language, yet the Christmas story in the Bible says Mary *pondered* all the events surrounding her child's birth.

It certainly makes sense that Mary would ponder. After all, she had encountered an angel who told her that she was about to have a baby. She knew that this birth was breaking acceptable behavior and social norms. She also had been told that she was specially chosen by God to bear a king, the Son of the Most High.

Then, after the birth, where there was only a manger for a crib, she had received visitors from the east who brought gold, frankincense, and myrrh. Shepherds came to see her child and told her stories of angels appearing to them in the field.

There was probably a lot of pondering going on with other people in the biblical Christmas drama, as well.

Zechariah had been filled with fear and trembling when he encountered the angel who told him of his future son, John, later known as the Baptist. When Zechariah learned that he would be literally speechless until his son was born, he had a lot to ponder. Why were he and his family chosen for such a vision and blessing? He was already old. What kind of father could he be? What kind of life would his child have since his birth was obviously very special to the holy God? What kind of training and nurture would he need to offer to this special child?

Mary's cousin, Elizabeth, too, had a lot to ponder. The hope she had long cherished (and almost given up on) was now going to be fulfilled. She was going to be a mother. Except that now she was getting on in years. Would she live long enough to see her child grow up? Would she be able to keep up with the child? Would the child be frustrated that she wasn't as young as the mother of his friends? Would she be an adequate mother and give her child the guidance he needed to be a person God would be proud of?"

And then, there's Joseph. First, he discovered that his future wife was already pregnant—which wasn't in his plans. And then in a dream, an angel told him not to worry—that this child was God's doing, that Mary's son was going to save people from their sins.

He definitely had a lot to ponder. Why did *his* wife have to be the one chosen by God? How was he going to parent this son who was not even of his blood? What in the world was God expecting him to do with or for the baby?

Joseph knew that he did not know how to teach his son how to save others from their sins. What was to be his role in preparing this son for his God-appointed responsibilities? How

Pondering

was this child going to affect his and Mary's relationship? After having the Son of the Most High, would she want to give him his own sons and daughters?

When the shepherds came and told Mary about their own special visitation from the angel, she began believing even more strongly that she and her Son would have special roles in the future. Did she have even a glimpse of how they would affect the history of the world? Did she begin to be scared for her child? Was she overwhelmed with the immensity of the job which God had given her? Perhaps so. But she treasured all the words of the shepherds and pondered them in her heart.

Pondering seems to be holy activity. And yet, how often do I ponder the things of my life? I may worry, I may stress, I may ignore…but do I ponder?

Pondering seems to have about it a sense of considering events with calmness, a way of looking at an event from several different angles, knowing that each angle is both accurate and inadequate. Pondering seems to contain a sense of knowing and yet not knowing. There is almost a sense of both "this is what I know now" and "I'm open to knowing yet even more today, tomorrow, during my life."

Pondering also seems to require silence and apartness. This part of pondering may be difficult to do…especially during the holiday season. There is always something more to do—more shopping, more wrapping, more baking, more e-mails, phone calls, cards to write. There are also the extra celebrations… special services, special parties, additional school events. There are television specials and musical programs and decorating, and seasonal traditions like riding around looking at tacky Christmas lights with friends and loved ones.

Pondering can also bring a measure of anxiety. If I stop in the midst of all the holiday chaos to actually think about God's activities in my life, I may be afraid of what I or God will find. I may be scared that God will ask me to change who I am, what I do, or how I live my life. I may be afraid that my carefully designed world of work, home, friends, and family may be totally disrupted. Look at what happened to Elizabeth, Zechariah, Mary, and Joseph!

And yet, can I honestly believe that Mary, Elizabeth, Zechariah, and Joseph would have had it any other way? Would they have given up their encounter with God and its ensuing results if they had known at the time what they learned later? Maybe what happened to them *was* risky…but what an outcome! And certainly, the impact of the intervention with God continued to make itself real as they pondered the past, the present, and the future.

The intention to ponder is well worth it. Time spent thinking about how God has and is interacting with me is the most wonderful gift I can give to myself and receive from God.

I will take time to ponder wherever and whenever I can: in the car line at school, sitting at my computer, taking a shower, folding clothes from the dryer. I will take time to ponder when I first wake up and just before bed, while baking or waiting for a concert to begin, when wrapping presents…even while taking out the garbage. I will enjoy this special, special gift!

How Many Tears Does It Take to Decorate a Christmas Tree?

There are tears of joy—
   for love
   for friends
   for family.

There are tears of grief—
   for lost loved ones
   for dreams deferred
   for things changing.

There are tears of anxiety—
   what if she...?
   what if he...?
   what if I...?

There are tears of forgiveness—
   for hurts released
   for damage remembered
   for mistakes, errors, and sins.

There are tears of frustration—
   for answers that will not come
   for apathy from our brothers and sisters
   for busy-ness that un-connects us.

There are tears for no reason—
  that cleanse
  that release
  that sparkle on the tree.

How many tears does it take to decorate a Christmas tree?
  Buckets and buckets;
  Made brilliant in God's love through the Christ Child;
  Filled with prisms of grace in the hope of Jesus Christ.

Gray Christmas

I painted the living room Let It Rain gray. I had decided that since Emmet and I were the only people in the house most of the time, I'd redo everything.

The grandchildren were long past the age when I needed to keep breakable items out of reach. They now remembered to wipe their feet before they came into the house during their rare visits. And even the dog had died so I no longer had to constantly clean up dog hair and paw prints.

I had already painted the hall Uncertain Gray and the kitchen cabinets Storm Cloud gray. The new colors were set off beautifully with all the white trim and the new white linen draperies that now hung at the windows. I had studied decorating magazines and watched shows about renovating houses. I knew that gray was the color of choice these days. I decided that I wanted to be current in my home. The past was the past. So there!!!

Our home was truly a house for adults now. I wanted it to look like that. I gave to Salvation Army all the little kid toys that

I'd kept for the grandchildren. I kept puzzles for older children, but we no longer needed the animal puzzles with ten pieces or the alphabet and U.S. States map puzzles. I decided that I could not part with certain games, however, even though the children preferred computer games. On occasion, I could entice them to play a board or card game with me.

So, I was engaged with my total house redo. I took the family room furniture to the upholsterer. I chose a beautiful Granite Peak gray washable fabric for the sofa with coordinating fabrics of Foggy Gray/Steely Gray/Online stripes for the chairs. I used other colors in my decorator pillows because I had learned from my research that everything should not match. I reframed all the family photos in black frames with white mats. I kept only the lamps that looked fresh after I changed the shade.

Bit by bit, the house was changing. I pulled out Emmet's mother's pewter collection and displayed it. The patina on those pieces looked beautiful against the Moon Mist gray of the dining room walls. I was pleased with what I had accomplished.

Emmet was not so sure. He disliked change. He thought the house was comfortable before I started "messing" with it. He loved seeing the pictures the youngest granddaughter had drawn directly on the walls. He liked seeing the torn sofa cushions where the dog had "dug" for lost bones.

He said that he felt like he was now living in a decorating show which delighted me—until I realized that for Emmet, that was not a good thing. He detested the beautiful new lush bathroom towels because he had just gotten the old frayed blue ones "broken in good."

I walked around my house and admired all the work I had done. My house was truly beautiful and coordinated…finally after all these years!

I was pleased with myself. I couldn't wait to show everything off during the holiday season. I began dreaming of how I would decorate the house. I knew for sure that I'd not pull out all the decorations that we'd accumulated over the years. The kindest description I could give for some of them was tacky. I decided to be very discerning about what items I would display.

When I went to the stores, I was overwhelmed with the displays of Christmas ornaments and decorations. Rows and rows of ornaments were color-coordinated or displayed by themes: Southwestern anyone? Ballerinas? Snowmen? Tropical paradise? Star Wars?

No, no, no. This was not what I wanted in my beautiful home. I looked at a row of black/white/silver ornaments. I finally decided that I'd get two dozen silver bells and intersperse them with any white ornaments I already had.

I bought all new white lights. I was tired of trying to untangle lights from previous years only to discover that some of the bulbs had burned out. I stocked up on red wrapping paper. I decided that I'd wrap every present in red paper tied with a large silver bow. I could just picture the tree surrounded by mounds of presents.

I awoke in the night—a regular occurrence—and pictured my house at Christmas, how glamorous it would be. I lay in bed and made up lists in my head as I planned my decorating process. I smiled as I filled my imagination with rooms that could easily appear in any of the decorating magazines that I studied so diligently.

Then, one night, I sat up straight in bed. Who is going to *see* my masterpiece? I realized that I had not talked with the children or grandchildren about when they were coming for the holidays. I had not thought about who Emmet and I could invite to our home during the season. I needed people to come to see what I had done. I wanted them to appreciate all the changes I had made.

I turned on the lamp beside my bed, picked up my clipboard and pen, and began making a list of people I wanted to invite to our house. Emmet, being Emmet, slept through all my planning efforts after he rolled away from the light. That man had no idea what went into planning a beautiful Christmas!

I didn't have many names written down before I turned off the light, but I knew that I would certainly think of more people in the days to come. Although we had not even celebrated Thanksgiving yet, it was never too early to begin planning invitations for Christmas gatherings.

I contacted the children to see when they thought they would come for the holidays. As usual, they did not know what their plans were except that Emmet and I would be on our own for Thanksgiving. Each family was going to spend Thanksgiving with the in-laws.

I was relieved. That meant I could put away all my fall harvest decorations and begin decorating for Christmas a bit earlier than I usually did. However, the fake pumpkins, large and small, with all their shapes and colors looked magnificent against my new gray color scheme. Those pops of orange were inspired, if I do say do myself.

I sent out a couple of e-mail messages to friends to invite them over in December for morning tea and muffins. Other than that, I decided that I'd surely find people to invite to the house. I put the list aside. I had more important things to think about. Should I put a fat tree in the front window or a skinny one? How would I decorate the front porch? I wanted elegant but not expected.

If I put something *on* the front door, it would need to blend with my Let It Rain gray walls when the door was opened. Would I do something *beside* the door? Candles? Garlands? Lanterns? Live or fake greenery?

Oh, there were so many decisions to make!

Emmet just sat in his chair watching television and let me dream my dreams. He had learned years ago that when I began with one of my "projects," the best thing for him to do was to stay out of the way. (Otherwise, he might get pulled into helping me.)

I really enjoyed decorating the house. It was fun to keep moving fake greenery until I had just the effect I wanted on the mantle. I edited all our old ornaments, using only white and silver ones.

I was especially partial to the crocheted snowflakes that my grandmother made before she passed away and I added a few clear glass ornaments that friends had given me. I had long since given my grown children their particular ornaments—the silver balls that my mother had given each of them at Christmas, the tiny trumpet for one and a saxophone for the other, the pilot bear for the son who wanted to fly planes, the dream catchers they'd made at summer camp, the school photos that I'd framed and hung on the tree, the unique ornaments they'd created in kindergarten.

When I finally completed my decorating, I was pleased with the results. My house looked like it never had before. It was elegant and sophisticated. Just what I'd envisioned.

I still had not heard from our children about their Christmas plans but the grandchildren had sent messages for what they'd like as presents from Emmet and me.

Unfortunately, their wish lists did not lead to gorgeous red-wrapped packages under the tree—gift cards and money don't really take up much space. I wouldn't have my pile of beautiful red boxes but the gift cards wrapped in silver and clipped to the tree kept things picture perfect.

The friends we called to come over for dessert already had plans with their own families. Some had tickets for various holiday concerts or dramatizations. We watched our mailbox for invitations but soon realized that people just did not entertain as they once had.

So, I turned on our tree lights every night, drank a cup of spice tea, and played Christmas music throughout the house. At least I could enjoy imagining sitting in a picture of *Better Homes and Gardens* or *Southern Living*!

Our children, who all live out of town, finally let us know their Christmas plans. Our son's family was staying at home since his wife had to work on Christmas Eve and he had to work on the day after Christmas. They said they were planning on a quiet day at home with their children. They looked forward to seeing us sometime in January when their lives settled down a little bit. Our daughter's family had decided to visit her husband's parents to celebrate Christmas with parents, siblings, and cousins.

I sat on my newly-reupholstered sofa in the family room and began to cry. Emmet, who was sitting in his chair, tried to comfort me by telling me that our children loved us but they had their own lives now. I wailed that we had our own lives, too, and I wanted to share it with them in our beautiful home.

Emmet just listened and wisely allowed me to cry. Later, he brought me a cup of tea and two cookies. (I took care not to drop any crumbs on the furniture.)

When I finished my tea, I walked from room to room, repeating to myself the hues of gray that I had used: Let It Rain, Uncertain, Storm Cloud, Granite Peak, Foggy, Steely, Online. I said the words again: Let It Rain, Uncertain, Storm Cloud, Granite Peak, Foggy, Steely, Online. The words seeped into my spirit just like fog moves into low spots. Everywhere I looked in my house, it was gray. Gray!!!

I began to look inside myself and realized that I was gray inside, too. Did I get lost in paint rather than looking for the radiance of a love that is always there? Did I believe that in fixing up my exterior surroundings that my life would be beautiful, elegant, and sophisticated?

In trying to redo my house, was I trying to let go of so much that was important to me? Did I miss the children and their laughter so much that I had to get rid of the things that reminded me of them? Was I so involved in creating a picture-perfect house that I forgot that life is messy?

I went out in the front yard and looked up. Even the sky turned gloomy. Rain clouds threatened around the house, but they never emptied themselves onto our parched grass. They just covered any night lights in the sky. I could see no moon or stars. Where was the light of the heavenly hosts? Where were the shepherds who were eager to share their vision? I dropped down on the steps and let the tears flow some more.

Emmet and I decided to make the best of our very bleak Christmas. We went to the candlelight Christmas Eve service at church. Even though it was very beautiful, I was despondent because on every pew sat families who were together for the holiday.

On Christmas Day, we cooked our favorite meal—potato soup and cornbread. I served it on my Christmas china but it still didn't seem very festive. Emmet gave me a pair of earrings and I gave him some new fishing equipment. We napped and watched a little television.

As I got ready for bed that evening, I was still feeling very gray. I know there's a Christmas song about having a blue Christmas. More like gray, I thought.

Then, just before I climbed into bed, I pushed aside the white draperies and looked out the window. A bright star peeked through the clouds. As I watched, the clouds parted and the star became brighter and brighter. Suddenly, the light from that special star began to shine deep inside of me. I felt it fill me up to overflowing.

I closed my eyes and heard or felt or imagined…I don't know exactly what it was…but I heard a warm, caressing voice saying, "I love you more than you can imagine. In my presence is the fullness of joy. Your sense of loss is part of life itself. The dark of the night precedes the grays of the dawn. And then comes the sun. The sun reminds you of the light of the Son whose birth the Church just celebrated while you were busy decorating your house."

I stood at the window for a few minutes, watching as the clouds hid the star again. Emmet asked me if everything was okay.

"Oh, yes," I said softly. "Everything is good. Very good. Merry Christmas, my love."

I climbed into bed beside him, turned off my light, and drifted into a dream—a dream filled with twinkling stars, bright colors (decidedly not gray), laughing children…and amazing grace that saved a decorating fool like me.

If This Were Not a Special Time of Year

If this were not a special time of year, there would be…
No Christmas trees
No nativity sets
No familiar carols and silly songs
No candles

This special time of year brings for some…
Emptiness
Despair
Grief
Isolation

Because this is a special time of year, there is…
Hope in the darkness
Waiting with assurance
Peace amidst chaos
Faith and strength to endure

Thank God this is a special time of year.

The Journey

Even at their ages, Matthias and Hannah still had to join others on the road between Nazareth and Bethlehem to be counted in the census.

The trip was tiring and monotonous. Hannah began paying attention to one young woman who reminded her of own daughter, who was also with child. She overheard her say to the man beside her, "Oh, husband. I am so tired. My back hurts. I am exhausted from sitting on this donkey for such long hours. Help me down so I can walk alongside of you for a while. This baby is kicking hard and maybe if I walk, I can find some comfort."

The man helped the mother-to-be to her feet. He stood by her as she regained her balance. Lines of worry crossed his forehead.

Hannah reached out and touched the young woman's arm. "I could not help but overhear your words to your husband," she said. "My name is Hannah and my own daughter, too, is with child. If I can help, please let me know."

The woman smiled a weak smile. Even so, her face seemed to glow. "Thank you. You are kind," she said. "I am Mary." She turned to the man with her. "This is my husband Joseph." She wiped her eyes with the back of her hand. "This is our first child. I am glad to know that you are near."

Hannah rejoined Matthias and left the couple alone, but she decided to keep a close watch on Mary and Joseph.

Joseph knew that Mary's time was very near…and that they still had much distance to cover before they arrived in Bethlehem.

The journey had been tedious. It could not have come at a worse time. As they walked in front of the donkey, Joseph mused to himself. "I wish the dream I had about Mary was as fresh for me today as it was when I first dreamed it. I learned that Mary was pregnant and I knew that I was not the father, but I care deeply for this young girl and wanted to do the honorable thing by her.

"I decided I would quietly put her away. I could have had her stoned, but I could not abide the thought of my sweet Mary…I cannot even finish that thought. It is too painful.

"Then I had the dream where the angel told me, 'Joseph, son of David, do not be afraid to take Mary as your wife, for the child conceived in her is from the Holy Spirit. She will bear a son, and you are to name him Jesus, for he will save his people from their sins' (Matthew 1:20-21).

"At the time, the dream seemed so real. I believed that the child Mary is carrying was truly sent to me by God. How that happened I cannot explain but I was certain that I would become the father of this son and raise him according to the prophets' teachings. I would teach him how to be a good carpenter. I would be a good father to the boy.

"But now…now, I'm not so sure. We've been walking along this road. I'm tired. I remember the disorientation we experienced when it became evident that Mary was with child. I remember how our neighbors whispered about us and some even scorned us.

"We certainly did not tell them that we each had been visited by angels. They did not and do not understand what is happening to us. *We* do not really understand what is happening to us.

"Where are you, God? Aren't you supposed to be taking care of us? Why do we have to walk this long journey from Nazareth to Bethlehem just at the very time when this child you tell me is yours is to be born? I don't understand. I feel as if you have been feeding us with bread of fatigue and filling our cups with tears. Mary certainly is weepy but I've been told that women can get this way when they are pregnant. O God, shine your face on us that we may be saved."

The couple continued to walk along, drinking water from their bag and eating a little bread when they stopped to rest. They shared food with some of their companions—Matthias and Hannah, as well as other travelers.

Each family provided what they could: bread, wine, figs, cheese, or whatever other meager items they may have had. The women travelers were especially kind to Mary because they could see how uncomfortable she was.

Mary did not complain aloud but she pulled into herself with her thoughts. She was ready for this baby to be born but she certainly did not want her son to be born on the side of the road. She too wondered about the visit from the angel. Was it truly real? Had she only imagined it?

As she walked, Mary tried to remember all the angel's words to her. "Greetings, favored one!" he had said. "The Lord is with you. Do not be afraid, Mary, for you have found favor with God. And now, you will conceive in your womb and bear a son, and you will name him Jesus. He will be great, and will be called the Son of the Most High, and the Lord God will give to him the throne of his ancestor David. He will reign over the house of Jacob forever, and of his kingdom there will be no end" (Luke 1:28-33).

For nine months, Mary had had a lot to think about. On the journey, she knew that she had no more clue about her future than any other mother has about the future after discovering she is pregnant. As the miles passed, Mary wondered, "Why was I chosen for this responsibility? Do I believe that I have been honored or punished? What does it mean to be the mother of the Son of the Most High? What is going to happen between Joseph and me? How in the world do you train someone to become the heir to the throne of David? What is God asking me to do? *Why* is God asking me to do this? Is there any way to say *no* to God? Where is God now? Is God on this road with us? I don't feel the presence of the Most Holy One. I simply feel weary and weepy."

And then the thought crossed Mary's mind that giving birth to the Son of the Most High might mean the circumstances for the birth would be vastly different than what they actually turned out to be. Having the Son of God on the side of the road or even in a barn? Outrageous! Mary wondered again if she had had some fantastic dream and that her understanding of the specialness of her baby was only a figment of her imagination. She knew that she already desperately loved her son but she was confused about so much else.

Mary remembered the laughter of the neighbors. She had many moments when she wondered where God was. She would sometimes walk away from the village so she could look at the shepherds in the far field. She well understood the psalmist's plea to God, the Shepherd of Israel. She yearned for God's might to save her and her family. But at times, she felt that God had turned away.

After a while, Mary asked Joseph to stop once again so she could rest. She looked up at her husband with both fear and faith in her eyes. Joseph realized that the baby's movements were likely making Mary very uncomfortable.

He gazed at her with a full heart. He pleaded with God using the ancient words of the psalmist. "Holy One, let your hand be upon the one at your right hand, the one whom you made strong for yourself. Then we will never turn back from you; give us life, and we will call on your name" (Psalm 80: 17-18).

As he helped Mary settle once again on the donkey, she said with tears in her eyes, "My dear husband, I must believe that with you and God, this journey will turn out okay. God will give us life in the form of our son, a boy whom we'll call Jesus. Beyond that, I do not know what the future holds for us, but

I know that God's face will shine on us. We'll see God's light when we first look at the face of our baby boy. We will be saved because of who God is."

Matthias and Hannah chatted with the couple as they traveled on the road. They sensed that something was special about Mary and Joseph.

Yes, they were obviously country people. Yes, they were tired. Yes, Mary was especially anxious because she knew that her time was near. Yes, they seemed distracted at times.

But there was something…something about this couple as they walked toward their future.

The Gift

The kings brought gold, frankincense, and myrrh.
The drummer brought his rat-a-tat-tat.
The angels brought messages of glory.
The shepherds brought awe and curiosity.

What do I bring?
I bring brokenness
I bring anxiety
I bring yearning

My gifts are given so the Son of God will in turn give
wholeness
peace
a place in the kingdom

My gifts are selfish
But are graciously accepted and cherished
For they are real
They come from the depths of my soul

For such is our Savior
King of Kings,
Prince of Peace,
Creator of the Universe,
Holy Comforter.

The Perfect Christmas

The tree looked beautiful with white lights, white snowflakes, and white ornaments. I placed white poinsettias and amaryllis blooms in various displays, along with fresh greenery and tiny red balls tucked here and there. The decorations in the house were simple yet elegant. My décor was not cute—just designed for beauty and taste.

Everything was going to be perfect this year—all in white with touches of red. For once, I would make a Christmas that could show up in a Martha Stewart magazine.

Of course, I still displayed most of my nativity sets because of their international appeal. My collection was the envy of several of my acquaintances. I made sure to invite them to my party so they could drool!

I had already sent out invitations to my open house drop-in and sent in my acceptances to at least one holiday party for each weekend prior to Christmas. My work colleagues and I planned to celebrate on a Tuesday evening for our office party because everyone was too busy on the weekends. I was going to a Christmas music matinee one Sunday afternoon and to the Nutcracker Ballet on another Sunday, in addition to all the parties.

I bought the most extravagant gifts I could find and anticipated that I would receive equally luxurious gifts. We givers and receivers would mentally determine which one of us had spent more money on the other. I knew that I would win most if not all those comparisons.

My holiday season was looking great. I was going to be busy and engaged with all the special events. I was excited.

The party season was everything I hoped it would be. There was lots of good food, laughter, and gorgeous clothing. The holiday music was happy and the decorations at each party were even more wondrous than at the last one. They were, as the kids say, awesome. I could tell that a lot of decorators and caterers had been very busy. They must have had very lucrative business this holiday season. Everything was a feast of celebration and competition. At each party, it seemed that the host had more unusual food, more important people, and more sparkle than the previous one. This was turning out to be the best Christmas ever.

My party was the highlight of the season…according to my best friend, Mattie. She said that my menu exceeded the aspirations of every other hostess that year. My decorations were over the top in their elegant simplicity. My international nativity sets were a collector's dream. My guests were people with power and prestige in our community. Those who were not on my guest list were envious.

Everything was impeccable. How marvelous for me!

There was just one last party of the season, and it was on Christmas Eve. One of my neighbors invited all the neighbors every year for a vegetable soup and cornbread supper.

Compared with all the other parties I'd attended, this one sounded like a real snooze fest. I did not usually go to this gathering but this year…what the heck! I'd been having such a good time everywhere, maybe this party would be better than I anticipated.

It took me a while to decide what to wear. A sequined sweater seemed too fancy for vegetable soup. I hoped this was not one of those "Ugly Christmas Sweater" parties.

My leather jeans could be just the thing. I would certainly be noticed in them, but they were still, after all, jeans. I finally decided on a crisp white blouse with a red cashmere sweater thrown casually around my shoulders. I finished off the outfit with diamond stud earrings, a gorgeous necklace that sparkled with chocolate diamonds, rubies, sapphires, and emeralds, and only three bracelets. I didn't want to be too flashy!

Since the evening was mild, I decided to walk. I imagined the comments that people would say about how great I looked. Every woman would be envious and every man…well, I won't say what might be going through the heads of those guys! I hummed Jingle Bells as I walked.

Suddenly, I was knocked down. My face was on the sidewalk. A rough hand grabbed my neck. I thought I was going to be strangled to death but, no, the thief wanted my necklace. He ripped it off, leaving scratches on my neck. He pulled my arm behind my back until I heard a crack. He jerked my bracelets off, kicked me in the side, and ran off.

Suddenly, I realized that I was not afraid or hurting or concerned about losing my necklace or bracelets. I was in a light-filled room with whitewashed walls and beautiful windows filled with pieces of stained glass. The colored glass didn't really make a picture, just prisms of reds and blues and greens.

I noticed there were farm animals moving around: goats, cows, sheep, and some chickens. And then people began to come into vision. I could not discern any faces. I had the impression that I did not know any of them. Some of them appeared to be the caretakers of the animals. Others had on fancy garb, especially headdresses, fancier than any I'd seen at any of the parties I'd attended.

Finally, a young man came to me. He lifted me up to a sitting position. He gently moved my arm and I realized that although it was broken, amazingly, it did not hurt.

The young man looked at me with warm brown eyes. Normally I would not have allowed someone dressed as shabbily as he was to touch me but for some reason, I was not afraid.

At that moment, I heard his voice. I cannot describe the beauty of it. It was not deep like a man's voice, nor was it high like a woman's. It was…ethereal. It was as if butterflies could speak. It was gentle and loving.

He said, "Why do you build your life on bigger and bigger parties? Why do you invest your time and energy in things that glitter but have no substance? Why do you forget?"

The next thing I knew a neighbor whose name I did not

know was kneeling beside me on the sidewalk and shouting, "Call 9-1-1!" Another neighbor brought a blanket to cover me until the ambulance arrived. Still another one, Lydia, rode to the hospital with me and waited until my broken arm was set and my abrasions treated with antiseptics and ointment. The hospital personnel wanted me to stay overnight in the hospital for observation, but I refused. I wanted to go home.

Joe, the husband of the couple who was hosting the party, came and picked Lydia and me up. He dropped Lydia at her house and then said, "Maria and I were talking. We don't think it's safe for you to be by yourself this evening. You may have a concussion. We want you to stay with us tonight."

My head was now hurting so badly I did not have the strength to argue with him. I let him lead me into his house. It smelled heavenly.

All evidence of the party had been cleared away, but the aroma of the vegetable soup still filled the air with comfort and joy. Maria asked if I'd like to try to eat some. I whispered *yes* as I lowered my eyes. I knew I looked disgusting, but I didn't care.

Maria brought me a bowl of soup. I'd never tasted anything so delicious. No canapés or crepes or eggnog had ever been as welcome as that pottery bowl with bits of carrots, beans, corn, and beef.

After I had eaten, Maria suggested that I come to the family room and lie on the couch. She wrapped a soft quilt around me. As I settled into the warmth, I noticed the tree with construction paper ornaments and small photos of their children. There were also kindergarten handprints and other ornaments obviously made by children. However, since there no children in the house as far as I could tell, I asked Maria about her family.

She told me that they had three married kids who were with their other families on this Christmas Eve. All their children, their spouses, and their seven grandkids had been with them over Thanksgiving. They had enjoyed having all the family around the table.

Trying to be polite, I said that she and Joe must really miss having their children at their home on Christmas Eve. Maria looked surprised. "Not at all. We'll still have a baby here this evening."

I guess I looked puzzled. I had not heard a baby crying nor had I seen any baby items such as high chairs, baby toys, or bouncy things. Seeing my confusion—I guess—Maria smiled.

"Jesus the Christ Child is joining us this evening."

"What?"

"You know, tonight is when we celebrate God's becoming human, one of us."

"Oh, yes. I forgot."

Joe spoke up for the first time. "You forgot? That's what Christmas is all about."

I shook my head. "Not in my world. Christmas is about parties, getting and receiving the right gifts, and attending special concerts and ballets. Christmas has nothing to do with God."

Maria and Joe looked at each other and Joe said, "Here, listen to this." He opened a Bible and began to read. "In those days a decree went out from Emperor Augustus that all the world should be registered" (Luke 1:1).

He looked up at me. I guess my face told him that I had a general recollection of the story, so he continued reading. He got to the part that said, "While Mary and Joseph were in Bethlehem, the time came for her to deliver her child. And she gave birth to her firstborn son and wrapped him in bands of cloth, and laid him in a manger" (Luke 1: 6-7).

"Oh yes," I said. "I know this part. I have a stellar collection of nativity sets. I have them from Kenya, Laos, Peru, Mexico, Israel, and many other places."

Maria looked at me with compassion. "Yes, having nativity sets can be very inspirational. They can remind us that God chose to become human, to join us as a vulnerable baby, so we could learn to live as God wanted us to."

I frowned slightly because this was not the response that I usually got when I told people about my nativity sets. Most wanted to know if I'd give or sell them my collection.

Joe continued reading. "In that region there were shepherds living in the fields, keeping watch over their flock by night" (Luke 1:8). He finished the entire story and told me I could find it again in the Gospel of Luke in the Bible.

We sat watching the lights twinkle on the tree. Even though it was getting late, I was not sleepy, and Joe and Maria seemed content to sit in the quiet with me.

Maria asked if I'd like a cup of their special Christmas peppermint tea and some date cookies. I nodded. While I lay there listening to her move around the kitchen, I was amazed that my arm was not hurting and that I was not sore all over my body. I figured the pain medications were doing their job.

When Maria brought me a plate of cookies, served, of course, on a Santa plate along with a mug of hot tea, I looked at both of them and said, "Can I tell you something and you'll not laugh at me?" I hardly knew these people but they seemed to genuinely care about me, so I decided to take the chance to tell them about the pretty place with the stained glass, animals, and the people.

They listened with encouragement shining in their eyes. Because they did not seem to think I was crazy, I decided I could tell them the rest. I said, "Just before I heard someone yelling to call 9-1-1, a man touched me and asked, 'Why do you build your life on bigger and bigger parties? Why do you invest your time and energy in things that glitter but have no substance? Why do you forget?'"

A calm silence descended on the room. I knew that Joe and Maria were allowing the questions to resonate in each of us. I was not uncomfortable, just a bit confused. I waited to hear what they would say.

Eventually, Maria said, "I think the questions you heard were designed for you to figure out the answers for yourself. All I can say is to remember that the God who created you is a God of steadfast love. God's grace and mercy surround you every moment of every day. We remember this night that God chose to become one of us to show how powerful that love is. What more might you need?"

With that Joe and Maria wished me a good night sleep, told me to call them if I needed them, and left me in my little nest on their sofa. I went to sleep staring at the handmade star on the top of the Christmas tree. Just before I dropped off, I heard a voice whispering, "Be not afraid."

The next morning Joe and Maria took me home. I kept in touch with them and told them I was still pondering the questions. They would smile and say, "You'll figure it out."

By the next Christmas, I knew that something had shifted inside me. I was no longer interested in impressing anyone with parties or decorations. I really didn't want to go to all the holiday events. I chose only a few to attend.

I still planned to decorate my house. However, when I unwrapped my first nativity set, the unimaginable happened. I heard the Christmas Eve voice again. This time it said, "I love you, feed my sheep."

I placed that nativity set on its shelf. I began unwrapping another one and heard, "As I have loved you, love one another."

With the next set, I heard, "Read Luke 12:13-21."

This one made me arch my back, raise my eyebrows, and wonder *what in the world?* But by now, I'd had enough strange experiences to know that I'd better pay attention.

Maria had given me a Bible shortly after my stay with them on Christmas Eve and showed me the different books in it. I stopped unwrapping the nativity sets and went to get it. I opened it to the passage the voice had told me to read and discovered an amazing story about a guy whose crops produced abundantly year after year, so he built bigger and bigger barns to store the grain in. He said to himself, "Soul, you have ample goods laid up for many years; relax, eat, drink, and be merry" (Luke 12:19).

When I read those words, I hurled the Bible across the room. I felt as if my hands were on fire. I had thought something very similar to those words last year, the year of my perfect Christmas. I had certainly relaxed, eaten, drunk, and was very merry…until…until…the thief in the night stole my jewelry and…and…

With that, I sat down in my chair and sobbed. I had forgotten that Jesus loved me. I had forgotten the real purpose of Christmas.

I remembered the love of Christmas that I'd experienced at Joe and Maria's house. I knew that I never wanted to forget again. I understood that Joe and Maria had swaddled me so the Christ could come to me.

I sat with my memories and cleansing tears flowed. Eventually, I retrieved the Bible from where it had landed when I'd thrown it across the room. I wanted to see how the story ended.

As it happened, Jesus said in the Bible that the barn guy died that night. That happened to me last Christmas Eve. I died to the old me. I had just not realized it…until now.

Nothing will ever be the same.

Be Not Afraid

"Don't be afraid" is repeated over and over in the stories surrounding the birth of Jesus. The angel who told Joseph about how special Mary's baby was said, "Don't be afraid." An angel appeared to Zechariah, the father of John the Baptist, and told him about his wife Elizabeth's pregnancy, and told him, "Do not be afraid." The angel who appeared to Mary to announce that she was going to be the mother of Jesus told her, "Do not be afraid." And let's not forget the shepherds who were minding their own business when a host—a whole lot—of heavenly beings appeared to let them know that Jesus had been born. What did the lead angel say? "Don't be afraid."

Why were each of these people afraid in the first place? Why did the angel need to admonish each to "Be not afraid?"

Well, Joseph was afraid because his intended wife had turned up pregnant. He wanted to do right by her, so he was thinking about dismissing her quietly. He certainly wasn't thinking about marrying her. What a scandal!

Of course, he was afraid. What would his family say? What would the neighbors think? How would this affect his business? His betrothed had done something that could hurt him personally and professionally. Something beyond his control could have a major impact on his life.

Be not afraid.

Zechariah was doing his priestly duties at the altar, behind the Holy of Holies. He was taking his turn doing the things that were most sacred in God's sanctuary. This is a time when a priest really doesn't want to mess up. And yet, rather than being allowed to concentrate on his responsibilities, he was confronted by an angel.

Who wouldn't be afraid? What in the world was happening? Did Zechariah wonder if he was losing his mind? Today with his advanced age, he might wonder if he was experiencing acute dementia. What would his peers think? How could he fulfill his tasks? And then, when the angel said that he and Elizabeth were going to have a baby at this point in their lives, well…I imagine he was fearful that something expected of him might prove to be more than he could handle.

Be not afraid.

Mary was just hanging out in Nazareth when the angel Gabriel appeared. She was already betrothed to Joseph and was in the midst of planning her wedding. Then this angel appears… to a peasant girl!

Mary probably didn't have a lot of life experience in the first place. Having an angel show up, of all things, could be very frightening. And that angel had said, "Greetings favored one! The Lord is with you." The Gospel of Luke says that Mary was perplexed..." REALLY??? Then it goes on to say, "She pondered what sort of greeting this might be" (Luke 1:28-29).

What were Mary's options as she considered the sort of greeting she had just received? Was she afraid that she was going to be told she would die? Did she consider that she might be asked to do something really scary...oh, I don't know... something such as giving birth to the Son of the Most High? Did she ponder that she might experience significant loss or grief...especially since she was about to become pregnant and *not by her betrothed?*

She had just received some news that might be bad or... good. Was she afraid that the words she had just heard would change her life forever beyond her wildest imagination? Was she scared that her ordinary life was about to be interrupted in profound ways by the Holy God? She must have been, or Gabriel wouldn't have said, "Do not be afraid, Mary, for you have found favor with God and now you will conceive in your womb and bear a son, and you will name him Jesus" (Luke 1:30).

Be not afraid.

The shepherds were doing their jobs. They were not very respected by their neighbors, as shepherding was rather low on the ladder of respectable jobs. These folks were minding their sheep and their own business. They were used to being shunned or ignored. They certainly were not trying to call any attention to themselves.

And then, while dozing in the evening, they were startled awake by a magnificent light. All of a sudden, there was this angel and a host of heavenly beings. Talk about being scared!

Did they think they were about to be blamed for something they had not done? Did they think they had been caught sleeping on the job? Were they simply scared that something they'd never seen or experienced before was happening? Did they think that lightning was about to strike them dead?

What in the world might they have thought? Did they just want to do their job and be left alone? Did they feel that others didn't appreciate their contributions to their world? Did they feel that they were being asked or told to do something that was counter to their daily responsibilities?

Well, sorta. They were told to leave their jobs and go verify the angel's story. They were to leave the sheep—nothing a shepherd should *ever* do. But the angel told them, "Don't be afraid."

It seems that each of these people…Joseph, Zechariah, Mary, and the shepherds…had very real reasons to be afraid. And yet, an angel told each one not to be afraid. Easy to say and hard to do.

Joseph was told that Mary's child was God's doing. The angel said, "The child conceived in her is from the Holy Spirit" (Matthew 1:20). In other words, this is of God.

Zechariah was told by Gabriel, "I stand in the presence of God, and I have been sent to speak to you and to bring you this good news" (Luke 1:19). Gabriel was simply delivering God's message.

Mary was told, "You have found favor with God…The Holy Spirit will come upon you…Nothing is impossible with God" (Luke 2: 30-37). Once again, God was in the middle of what's happening.

The shepherds were told, "Glory to God in the highest," and they talked about "this thing…which the Lord has made known to us" (Luke 2:15). There went God again.

Every one of these "Be not afraid" statements was couched in the framework of God's actions. *God was present.* The things that were so out of the ordinary were God's doings. This was of God: *Be not afraid.*

Joseph, Zechariah, Mary, and the shepherds were just going about their everyday tasks. Each of them was shaken out of their complacency, their ordinariness by something that frightened them. They may have been scared silly. They may have begun to feel dysfunctional. Joseph, Zechariah, Mary, and the shepherds may have felt paralyzed for a bit. But hearing those holy words, "Be not afraid" got them moving…yes, in new directions from where they had thought their lives were going. But they lost their paralysis.

Joseph moved beyond his fear and took Mary as his wife and he named the child she bore Jesus.

Zechariah was literally speechless until his son was about to be circumcised. At that point, he moved beyond his fear, began praising God, and spoke prophecy about the Savior.

Mary immediately moved through her fear, and said, "Here am I, the servant of the Lord; let it be with me according to your word" (Luke 1:38).

The shepherds moved through their fear and made known what had been told them about the child and amazed everyone with whom they spoke.

Not being afraid is something every person yearns for. I don't want to hold onto fear for my family, my friends, my health, my community, my world, or even for myself. I want to live with freedom and joy, though I crave safety.

I DO NOT WANT TO BE AFRAID.

The Christmas message is that *with God, anything is possible.* Yes, I may be shaken out of my preconceived notions of how my own little world is to function. Yes, I may have to redefine what comfort looks and feels like. Yes, I may have to revisit some of my opinions. Yes, I may have to learn a new "normal" for my health or finances. Yes, I may have to risk my reputation as I've defined it. Yes, I may have to experience a conversion. And yes, the gospel swells with the message that God is with me, is ALWAYS with me, was with me even before I was born, and will be with me forever.

I *need* to hear, "Be not afraid." I *need* to know that life is surrounded by God's love, the Spirit's holy care, and Jesus's affirmation of being with us always. I *need* the Christmas message of "be not afraid." Sometimes the *only* thing I may be able to do is to stop in the midst of my fear and listen for angel voices singing, "Be not afraid."

The Christmas season calls me to not be afraid and get on with life as God is guiding me. And maybe, just maybe, I can join Mary by saying, "Here I am... let it be with me according to your word." And I take a deep breath...

Alleluia. Glory be to God.

Angelika's Christmas

Excerpt from Beth Lindsay Templeton, *Angelika's Journal: What You Can Do About Poverty and Hunger*, Avenida Books: 2014

December 1

Mama, my brother, and I have left our friend Barbara's house. We'd been staying there since we got evicted but we're not where I had in mind. We now live in a shelter for women and children. Thank goodness my brother is still little because if he was ten, he couldn't stay in the shelter with us and we would still be at Barbara's. This place really isn't so bad. The beds are comfortable. We share a room with another woman and her little girl. I like both of them because they're quiet and keep their part of the room clean just like we do. I can write in my journal again in peace and quiet. So long for now.

December 4

I'm having to change schools again because the bus that comes to the shelter goes to a different school. Who knows what will happen here?

December 7

I'm not going to write about school for a while. It's the same thing all over again so I'm just going to try to find other things to think about. Mama likes this place. Even though she's got a job, the people who run this shelter are working to help her find a better job. She goes to classes here in the evenings to improve herself. We are beginning to have a little hope. I hope we can stay for a long time.

December 10

I just found out that we can't stay here forever but that we can stay as long as Mama and we work on improving our situation. I'll try real hard to do my best at school. I'll help take care of my brother so that Mama can continue in her classes here. She seems to like what they are teaching her.

December 12

I brought a note home today for Mama. My teacher wants to have a "parent-teacher" conference with her. I don't know what to do. The conference is during the time when Mama is at work and she can't leave her job because she might lose it. And if she loses her job, we might not be able to stay in the shelter.

The teacher told all of us that if our parents cannot come at the time she suggests to let her know and she will try to work out something. The girl who sits beside me said the teacher met her mom at a coffee shop near where they live. That's really nice of the teacher. The only problem is that I don't want her to know that we live in the homeless shelter. I'll have to think about all this.

December 14

I'm still thinking about that stupid parent-teacher conference. I haven't given Mama the note yet. The teacher asked me about it and I told her that I forgot to pick it up off the table to bring it back to school. I told her that Mama had signed it, though. I don't usually tell lies but I don't know what else to do.

December 15

Mama could tell that something was bothering me. At first, I told her nothing was wrong but she looked so concerned and started crying about what a bad mama she was that I finally broke down and told her about the parent-teacher conference. She said for me not to worry. She would figure something out.

December 18

Mama met my teacher. I don't know exactly what happened. I know that she talked with the lady who works here at the shelter. Anyway, they worked out something and I'm glad they did. Mama said that my teacher can tell that I'm really smart. Even though I've only been in her classroom a little while, I am doing well. That made Mama happy. I'll work really hard now to make them all proud.

December 20

Today was our last day of school before the winter break. I'm sad because I was just beginning to figure out how this school worked. Oh, well.

December 21

Hey, living in this shelter at Christmas is pretty cool. Today a group from a church came here and gave us a Christmas party. We had all kinds of cakes and cookies. They had pretty napkins with holly on them. Mine was so beautiful, I didn't use it but brought it back to our room. I'm going to keep it in my journal. They gave us presents. The girls got things in the pink bags and the boys in the blue ones. They had bags for little kids and a few for some us of us older girls. I got nail polish, hand cream, and a pretty hair clip.

I showed Mama my presents and she smiled her thin smile and said, "That's nice." Before the party was over, she told my brother and me to come back to the room. I don't know why but we did as she asked us.

December 22

What do you know? We had another Christmas party. We got books and art supplies. Mama didn't even come to this party because she said she had a headache. This time we had pretty red punch and green cupcakes. This is fun.

December 23

Can you believe it? More people came to the shelter today for Christmas celebrations. This time it was a group of teenagers who sang Christmas carols. I was excited about the singing until I realized that one of the singers goes to my school. I hid so she wouldn't see me. I didn't come forward this time to get a present.

December 24

Today the shelter had its own kind of celebration. We gathered together to read the Christmas story and then we had a nice supper together. We sang some Christmas carols and then shared favorite Christmas memories. I told about the time we had a real tree and Santa Claus came and everything. I looked over at Mama and she had tears in her eyes. I asked her what her favorite memory was. She said it was the first Christmas after I was born. She felt like she and Mary, Jesus's mama, were sisters because they both had babies. Mama said she felt blessed. She said the words the angels said about be not afraid were very powerful for her that year. I liked that. That was a wonderful Christmas memory.

We all sat around just singing and talking quietly. The little kids, of course, were very excited and hoped that Santa Claus would find them at the shelter. Their mamas took them to bed while the rest of us sat around feeling warm and cozy and a little sad.

December 25

Today is Christmas. The little kids were screaming early because they found presents that Santa Claus had left them. Every kid had at least one present with his or her name on it. Some of them got big wheels, the girls got dolls with carriages. Others got board games or even game boys. Everybody got candy, fruit, and coloring books.

I didn't even go over to the tree because I was not expecting any presents there. I knew that Mama didn't have money for special treats like Christmas presents. But one of the ladies who works at the shelter called me over. She said, "Angelika, here's a present with your name on it." I looked at Mama who looked very surprised.

When I got to the tree, the lady handed me a very small box. My eyes got big. I think I mumbled thank you and then walked back over to sit with Mama and my brother, who was coloring. I very carefully opened the package. I didn't want to rip the paper or the bow. Slowly, slowly, I got the box unwrapped. In it was a beautiful watch! It was the prettiest watch I'd ever seen. And the time was already set on it so I knew exactly what time it was. It was 10:09 when I opened the present.

I looked at Mama and said, "Thank you." My mama began crying and left the room. I was puzzled and followed her to our room.

"What's wrong, Mama? This is the most beautiful present that I've ever received. I love it. Thank you."

Mama said, "That's just it. I didn't get you that watch. I couldn't afford something as nice as that. Somebody else gave you the best present you've ever gotten and it wasn't your mama. But it should have been. It should have been."

I began to take the watch off and put it back into the box. Mama saw what I was doing and said, "You stop that right this minute, girl. This is the nicest present you've ever gotten and just because your mama is feeling sorry for herself is absolutely no reason for you not to have nice things. You wear that watch with pride and joy. Jesus gave you that watch on his birthday. You just keep that love in your heart."

Then she said, "Angelika, my angel, my special baby, you hand me that watch." So I did. She took in it in her hand and closed it tight into her fist. Then she put her fist on her chest over her heart and she prayed, "Thank you, Jesus, for giving my angel this wonderful gift. Just as my hand is surrounding this watch, so my love is surrounding it and her life. May this watch remind her that every minute of her life is in your hands. When she looks at it, may she remember that her mama's love goes round and round her just like the little hands of this watch. Thank you, Jesus, for showing us your love on this special day. Amen."

Then she handed it back to me. I sat for a moment and then put the watch on.

If anyone ever asks me again what my favorite Christmas memory is, this is the one I'll share.

Season's Greetings!

*H*ow I love you! You please and delight me. I have given you my power so that you can do the work I am asking you to do. Because I have chosen you to represent me, I am supporting you, my beloved.

What is it I want you to do? I want you to teach and show everyone how to be righteous. I know that's an out-of-date word but what I want is for everyone to live in a healthy, whole, positive relationship with me and with each other. No, I don't mean behaving appropriately based on some kind of legal or ethical code. No, I don't mean impartial ministry to each other nor do I mean giving everyone his/her fair share.

What I do mean is peace, nonviolence, and wholeness. I want your saving works to be done quietly and patiently. And for God's sake—excuse me, *my* sake—don't act like a bull in a china shop as you work for righteousness.

I know, I know. It's common practice to give away old clothes or to pretend you don't see a homeless person on the street. But when you do these things, think of all my children who are weak and helpless. Remember all my bruised and wavering children who are victims or just about to be destroyed. Don't you be their oppressor, too, as you go about doing the work I've given you. I want you to bring about love and peace and justice for all my children in your community and in the whole world.

And when you care for my world and when you serve me, my blessed servant, then you, too, will grow. You won't be cast off like last year's model. You'll have me with you while we're showing and teaching people how to live—really *live*—with each other.

I love you. Now go out and serve my world in this holiday season and throughout the year.

God

The Best Christmas Gift

It was rare these days to receive an invitation in a hand-addressed envelope. Vivian opened it immediately and smiled. It announced the annual volunteer and staff covered-dish Christmas luncheon at Empower, the nonprofit where she volunteered. Vivian had not missed this event in all the ten years that she'd been volunteering. She immediately began thinking about what culinary masterpiece she would carry.

Deciding what to make would not be an easy task. Some of the older volunteers did not cook anymore and the younger folks often ran into a deli and bought something to bring.

And then, several volunteers Vivian worked with had developed food allergies. She would not make her famous macaroni cheese pie because Margaret was gluten and dairy-free. Her world-renowned pound cake was off Harold's list because he was diabetic. And Emily was vegan, for now.

Vivian wasn't worried, though. She put the invitation on her refrigerator door. She would continue to think about her food offering for the next couple of weeks until the party. She had plenty of time.

In the meanwhile, Vivian went to Empower to answer the phones on Tuesday mornings and to help a student with math for the high school equivalency exam on Thursday afternoons. Occasionally, she filled in at the day center for people who were homeless. There she handed out towels and shampoo.

The week before the luncheon, Vivian finally decided on what to make. She would prepare a big pot of vegetable soup along with gluten-free cornbread. She bought plastic soup bowls and soup spoons to take, too. The soup was hearty and nourishing and different from a casserole, salad, or dessert. Vivian knew that Margaret, Harold, and Emily would enjoy eating what she brought.

With that decision made, Vivian focused on getting ready for Christmas. Not only did she decorate her own home, she also made sure that her mother's apartment was festive. Even though Donna lived independently, she was no longer able to pull out the decorations or reach and bend to put them out.

Vivian always made a party out of the decorating process. She carried homemade cookies and a mix of Christmas music, so she and her mother could recreate some of their memories of Christmas past. They invited other residents in to celebrate with them, too.

Because her husband had loved eggnog, Donna made sure she bought some for the occasion. Even though William had long been dead, this time of year seemed to bring him alive again to his wife and daughter as they pulled out ornaments he had made. Donna shared stories with her guests as she told about William's various creations. They all toasted him with a glass of eggnog held high.

Donna first held up a clown that William made. "William used blocks of wood for the body, and he painted faces on the wooden heads," she said. "He learned to sew enough to make the arms and legs that he then stuffed with candies." Donna's face glowed when remembering him in his workshop. "William delighted in giving the clowns to children and to people in nursing homes during the holiday season."

Next she held up the nativity set that he made. "William cut Mary, Joseph, baby Jesus, the sheep, and the star out of wood. He put pegs in the bottom of each character so they could stand up in the display board where he had drilled holes." She demonstrated by placing the characters in their proper places. Then she showed how the entire set could be taken apart and stored easily after Christmas. She added, "William made several of these sets for family members and friends from church."

Donna lovingly cradled in her hands the star ornament that William had made for the children at church. "The minister gave William's stars to every child at the Christmas Eve service."

Her face lit up as she pulled out other ornaments William had made or collected. She delighted in her friends' reactions as they once again witnessed the love and delight that Donna and William had shared, especially in the Christmas season.

Vivian usually shed a few tears even while she smiled and chatted with her mom and her mom's friends. Yes, Christmas and this time with her mom and their memories of William were indeed special.

After everyone left the apartment, the two women looked around. Satisfied with what they had accomplished, they sat down to admire the twinkling lights and eat the remaining cookies. Donna poured them both a bit more eggnog and they settled in to chat.

Vivian brushed the crumbs from her lap. "Anything special happen this week?"

Her mother thought for a moment. "Well, the podiatrist made his once-every-three-month visit to the complex so I had my toenails clipped. Then, let's see. On Tuesday, I attended a piano concert offered in the community room. I went to Bible study on Wednesday afternoon." She shared some of the community gossip and her concern over the health of one of her friends. Donna smiled. "I had a good week. And now here is my daughter helping me get ready for Christmas! I am truly blessed."

Vivian told her mom about her time at Empower that week. Donna loved hearing stories of the various people that Vivian interacted with. She laughed about the guy who regularly proposed marriage to Vivian. She was saddened when Vivian told about some of the young parents who struggled so hard and still could not get out of the poverty they were trapped in.

When Vivian told her mother about the students she was tutoring, Donna stopped. "Have you ever heard from Susan?"

Donna knew that, over time, one young woman named Susan had become very important to her daughter. Vivian had worked with Susan several years before and had established a deep bond with the young woman.

But the relationship had not been easy. Life had been tough for Susan, and she led with her anger. In order to cope, she'd developed an attitude and foul mouth. Even so, she was determined to earn her high school equivalency so she could get some training to work in the medical field. She'd heard that you could make good money and that you could always find work.

But, the young woman thought she knew it all. No one could tell her anything. When someone tried to help, Susan might spew a lot of angry, colorful words. She kept her guard up because that's what she'd learned to do to survive her environment. Nevertheless, she kept coming back for tutoring.

Vivian began to notice that Susan only showed up when she knew that she would be there. Staff members said that Susan told them that Vivian was the only person who really "got" her.

Vivian pushed Susan hard when she needed it, especially when she wanted to give up. She also brought Susan little treats: a couple of cookies, a writing pen, a book about medical careers. Susan's rants became fewer in number, but she struggled with the lessons. Vivian cheered any incremental improvement and Susan always smiled… but not when she thought Vivian could see.

As time went on, Susan began to tell Vivian about her childhood and home life. Vivian listened in amazement at the strength that Susan demonstrated as she told what she had to do to survive the abuse, neglect, and fear in her life.

Susan also listened to Vivian as she told about her husband, children, grandchildren, and her mom. In some ways, Vivian became the stabilizing adult in Susan's life and Susan became the developing young adult that Vivian missed having around since her children were grown and lived busy lives. The two women's relationship developed even as the high school equivalency test skills crept along.

Then, one week, Susan had not come to meet with Vivian. She did not come the next week or the next. Vivian asked the staff if they'd heard anything but they, too, had lost contact. No one seemed to know where Susan was or what she was doing.

Ellen, the program manager, explained to Vivian that this can happen. "A person can be doing well and then life intervenes," she said. "A family member may make fun of the learning or feel threatened by it. An eviction can mean the bus line is no longer available. Maybe someone gets sick. Occasionally a person will be arrested." Ellen said they tried to contact program participants, but the unstable life of poverty often made that difficult, if not impossible.

Vivian grieved the loss of her time with Susan. She prayed for Susan every night and asked Donna to do the same. Even though she no longer spent time with the young woman, she thought of her frequently and hoped that she was able to reach her goal of getting her education, so she could have a better life.

But now, years had gone by with no news. "No, Mom," said Vivian to her mother. "I haven't."

Vivian told her mother about the upcoming volunteer and staff Christmas luncheon. She explained her dilemma about what food to take. When Donna confirmed the soup idea, Vivian smiled. She was still her mother's little girl and delighted in her approval.

When Vivian returned home, she updated her husband about all their holiday plans for attending parties, worship services, and special seasonal programs. She asked him to pick up postage stamps so she could mail her holiday cards. She knew that many people had stopped sending "real" cards but this tradition was one she vowed to maintain.

They discussed when they would be with various contingents of their family: children, siblings, grandchildren, nieces, and nephews. Vivian told Sam about her visit with her mom and how glad she was to share Christmas memories with each other and her mom's friends. She told Sam with a grin that her mom approved of the vegetable soup for the volunteer and staff covered dish lunch at Empower.

Even with all the holiday tasks, Vivian maintained her schedule at Empower. She knew that many people she saw there would never complain about being super busy during the Christmas season because they anticipated little or no holiday. Vivian asked her Sunday school class to help fill a basket with small treats that she could put in the lobby for people to have when they came to Empower, and she helped decorate the halls and offices of the various programs. She believed that she could provide a little bit of holiday cheer to people who had little and expected even less.

When the day for the luncheon arrived, Vivian decided to dress with all her holiday "accessories." She put on her Christmas bulb earrings, her holly turtleneck shirt with her red fleece over-shirt, and her black velour pants. She added red and white striped socks under her usual athletic shoes. She decided the reindeer antlers on her head were a bit much, so she left them at home.

She packed up her soup in the crock pot and gathered her bowls, soup spoons, and cornbread muffins.

When she arrived, Vivian was pleased to see Harold, Margaret, and Emily, along with other friends she'd made at Empower. The staff members, with their Santa hats, were especially cheerful and greeted the volunteers with big hugs and hearty thank yous. Everyone was amazed at the amount and variety of food. Many started with Vivian's soup and then cruised the buffet table later for other enticing dishes. And of course, desserts.

After everyone had eaten, Steve, Empower's administrator, stood up and asked for everyone's attention. "Before we begin our tradition of singing Christmas carols and songs, I have a special item I want to share. Vivian, will you please join me up here?"

Vivian looked at her friends with puzzlement on her face, but she stood and walked toward Steve. With a huge grin on his face, Steve announced, "This year Empower is honoring Vivian for her ten-plus years of service as well as for being one of Santa's top elves." He handed Vivian an "autographed" picture of Santa Claus. Everyone stood up and clapped and cheered. Vivian managed to squeak out a thank you and sat down with her face as red as Santa's coat.

When Vivian told Sam at supper about her award, he leaned over and kissed her. "You're *my* number one elf. Congratulations, honey."

While Vivian cleaned up the kitchen, she thought about the many people she had been blessed to know while at Empower.

She loved the staff with their strong commitment, their particular and personal quirks, and their passion for serving others. She thought of homeless Billy, who lived under a bridge and said he prayed for her every day; Patrice, who was a single mother who told about needing help with her rent because her ex had not sent the child support; and Mandy, who loved to laugh whenever she stopped by for a "visit;" as well as the many people whose names Vivian never knew or had forgotten.

And, of course, she thought of Susan. She prayed for all the people who were part of Empower as program participants, staff, or volunteers. She asked God to sustain each and every person and help her to be part of the answer to her prayers. With that, she finished wiping down the counter, hung up the dish towel, and went to watch a Christmas movie on television while Sam slept in his chair.

In the next week, Vivian and Sam enjoyed all the Christmas gatherings they went to. They decided that this was becoming one of their best Christmas seasons ever. They felt close as they held hands while listening to the Christmas cantata at church or sitting by the fire with the Christmas tree lights twinkling in the fire light. They enjoyed watching Donna when they all attended the nativity play the grandchildren were in. Vivian and Sam heard each other humming Christmas tunes at odd times of the day. They'd grin when caught sneaking in a package that they did not want the other to see. They were comfortable and warmly happy.

Then, on the night of December 23, the phone rang about 11:30 and Vivian answered it. Sam listened, trying to figure out who it was. He saw Vivian's face drain of color as her hand reached out for his, and heard her say, "We'll be right there."

Donna had fallen. Vivian and Sam drove immediately to the emergency department of the local hospital and the medical staff confirmed that Donna had broken her hip. They would do surgery in the morning.

Vivian held Donna's hand and rubbed her forehead to help Donna relax with the medications they had given her. Donna was woozy but was able to tell Vivian what had happened. "I fell when I was reaching for a glass in the kitchen. I'm so sorry I'm messing up your Christmas."

Vivian shook her head. "Mom, nothing is more important than you are. Besides," she said, "we can sing carols and read the Bible story wherever we are…even in the hospital."

She decided to stay with her mother, and told Sam to go home and call the rest of the family in the morning.

Sam nodded. "I'll be back with coffee and your toiletries and a change of clothes for you." Vivian wrapped her arms around her husband, told him how glad she was that he was her husband, kissed him, and sent him home.

A few hours later, Donna was taken into surgery, and Vivian dozed until Sam returned. She freshened up so that her mother would not be concerned about her.

Donna came through the surgery well and was returned to her room in a surprisingly short time. She slept off and on and the staff checked on her and began getting her moving as quickly as they could. Despite being still affected by the anesthesia, she wished everyone who came to the room "Merry Christmas."

Vivian asked Sam to go to her mother's apartment and pick up her favorite Christmas sweater along with her gown, robe, underwear, toothbrush, and face cream. She called the family to give them an update and to ask them to wait until Christmas Day to come by to see their grandmother. She wanted Donna to be in her Christmas sweater when they came so she would feel festive, despite being a patient.

All in all, Christmas Eve day was uneventful, but Vivian chose to stay again with her mom that evening. She sang Christmas carols to her mom as she drifted in and out of sleep. Then she recited as much of the Biblical Christmas story as she could remember.

Once Donna fell into a deep sleep, Vivian curled up in her chair, whispering the words from the Christmas story. "Fear not. Fear not." She wondered what the future held for her mom and if she would have to move and where would they move her and…what if…what if…

Finally, Vivian slept too.

The next morning both women were awakened early by a cheerful voice. "Merry Christmas, sleepyheads. Wake up. I'm here to take your vitals. Then we're going to get you up so you can see what Santa Claus left under your tree!"

Vivian slowly opened her weary eyes. She was vaguely irritated that someone would burst into the room like that—despite the fact it was Christmas Day. She reached for her glasses so she could read the woman's name tag, planning to complain to the supervisor about her.

She glared at the tag and a chill ran down her spine. SUSAN, it read. As Vivian's eyes focused, she blinked and then blinked again. Could it be?

"Susan, is that you?"

The nurse looked at Vivian and her face broke into a big grin. "Thanks be to God. It's my Vivian."

The two women met at the foot of the bed and hugged and hugged again. While she recorded Donna's blood pressure and other vital signs on the chart, Susan kept shaking her head and grinning. "I had no idea that Miss Donna was your mother since your last names are different. I want to talk with you but right now, I have other patients to tend to. I'll be back."

Vivian vigorously nodded yes as she watched Susan bustle out of the room.

Vivian helped Donna put on her Christmas sweater, combed her hair, and gave her mom lipstick to apply. When the family came in to check on "poor grandma" they were astounded to find their grandmother looking like a Christmas elf in her hospital bed. The children did not stay long because they realized that their Gran was tiring quickly, but they all felt better after seeing her so determined to get going again.

After all of the visitors left, Donna fell back asleep. The door opened slightly, and Susan waved to Vivian to come out into the hall so they could talk.

"When I left Empower, I was ready to quit trying. However, I kept thinking of you and how much you believed in me. I thought to myself, 'Vivian is not stupid and if she believes in me, then there must be more to me than I realize.'

"I moved away to live with relatives in another part of the state because I knew that staying where I was living at the time wasn't healthy.

"I enrolled in adult education and passed my high school equivalency exam. Then I trained as a Certified Nursing Assistant, which is what I am now. But I'm also enrolled in classes to become a medical technician."

Vivian's smile got bigger and bigger and tears pooled in her eyes as Susan related her story. When she finished, Vivian hugged her again. "I'm so proud of you. I KNEW you could do it!"

Susan looked right into Vivian's eyes. "Don't be afraid for your mom. She's doing well, all things considered. You took care of me when I needed it. Now I'll take care of her for you. Go home and rest. She'll be fine because I'm here."

As Vivian lay in bed that night with Sam, it occurred to her that even though her mother had broken her hip, God's love had been reinforced for each of them.

She turned off the light and smiled in the dark. As she drifted off to sleep in the relaxation of one who knows she is loved, she whispered to herself. "This is the best Christmas present ever."

Christmas Benediction

A child is born in Bethlehem who can give gifts beyond compare. I will take care of this child and bless him as he blesses me.

A star guided wise people to find this special child. I will find my own star and allow it to lead me on my God-birthed path.

Hope exploded in a crude abode which housed a new born baby, parents, and shepherds. I will nurture my fledgling hope so I can eagerly work for and await the promised new world of grace, love, peace, and joy.

May the deep spirit of Christmas fill my life to overflowing so I can go out into the world—singing, dancing, praising, and joining with others to live in a glorious new world where there is no fear, pain, or loneliness.

May the grace of the Lord Jesus Christ and the love of God and the fellowship and communion of the Holy Spirit be with me now and always.

Amen.

Acknowledgments

For a number of Advent seasons, the women of Fourth Presbyterian Church in Greenville, SC, asked me to preach an Advent Communion Service on the first Tuesday of December. This opportunity led to the challenge of writing sermons that addressed the season and yet were still unique. The journey that began years ago on that first Tuesday morning in December at Fourth Presbyterian Church influenced this book. Thank you, Presbyterian Women.

The process got pushed again when the Rev. Dr. Matt Matthews, a colleague in ministry as well as an accomplished author, issued a call for Christmas stories, poems, or snippets that might be included in a book he and a friend were thinking about. His project was never born but the story I wrote in response to that invitation began a tradition for me to write a Christmas story for my friends each year. Thanks, Matt, for planting that seed!

The many people whose path has crossed mine while at United Ministries as well as at Our Eyes Were Opened, Inc. certainly gave me material for some of the stories. I am forever grateful for the opportunity to have spent so many years with such wonderful people.

I have been blessed with a cloud of witnesses. Similarity to anything someone else has written is unintentional. If noted, please let me know so I can give proper credit.

I am an inveterate holiday decorator as well as consumer of home design magazines and shows. The colors mentioned in Gray Christmas came from Sherwin Williams color charts. I love Christmas and force myself not to begin decorating until the day after Thanksgiving! I am grateful to the explosion of home decorating ideas and guides.

My extended family will find familiar scenes and items mentioned in the stories. Thank for you for this rich heritage.

And to my husband Jim: You allow me to stay on my computer all day long, to be in my head figuring out a work challenge even when I'm sitting across the table from you, and to ask for shoulder massages with abandon. Additionally, you feed my creative spirit and my body with your cooking. You are truly my Christmas blessing. Remember, we began dating at Christmas!

Blessings to all.

Beth
October 31, 2017

About the Author

BETH LINDSAY TEMPLETON, Founder and CEO of Our Eyes Were Opened, Inc. is a public speaker, Presbyterian minister, retreat leader, and writer. A graduate of Presbyterian College and Erskine Theological Seminary, she worked for many years at United Ministries, a non-profit in Greenville, South Carolina, where she interacted with both "the have-nots" and "the haves." Since 2007, she has focused on a ministry with "the haves" so they can enlarge their thinking about people who live in poverty in order to reduce judgment and increase compassion.

Beth works with congregations, schools, universities, medical facilities, women's groups, civic groups, and businesses in Greenville and around the country.

She and her husband have three married sons and five grandchildren.

www.oureyeswereopened.org
beth@oewo.org

www.ingramcontent.com/pod-product-compliance
Lightning Source LLC
Chambersburg PA
CBHW071708040426
42446CB00011B/1976